KEYSTONES for READING

COMPREHENSION ▪ VOCABULARY ▪ STUDY SKILLS

Level F

Alden J. Moe, Ph.D.
Lehigh University

Sandra S. Dahl, Ph.D.
University of Wisconsin

Carol J. Hopkins, Ph.D.
Purdue University

John W. Miller, Ph.D.
Georgia Southern College

Elayne Ackerman Moe, M.Ed.
Carbon-Lehigh Intermediate Unit

MODERN CURRICULUM PRESS
Cleveland ● Toronto

Table of Contents

Lesson 1: **Word Histories** 1

Lesson 2: **Strictly American** 5

Lesson 3: **What's the Forecast?** 9

Lesson 4: **When the Earth Quakes** 13

Lesson 5: **Bridging the Gap** 17

Lesson 6: **Fortress or Luxury?** 21

Lesson 7: **Fads and Fashions** 25

Lesson 8: **Let the Show Begin** 29

Lesson 9: **Humble Papa Haydn** 33

Lesson 10: **It All Adds Up** 37

Lesson 11: **Circles of Terror** 41

Lesson 12: **Mountains of Fire** 45

Lesson 13: **Let the People Decide?** 49

Lesson 14: **Who's Afraid of a Number** 53

Lesson 15: **Artists Through the Ages** 57

Lesson 16: **Fun in the Summer Sun** 61

Lesson 17: **A Prehistoric Pair** 65

Lesson 18: **The Continents** 69

Lesson 19: **Unusual Facts About the United States** 73

Lesson 20: **The Longhorn Trail** 77

Lesson 21: **The Charles S. Wilson Fruit Jar Zoo** 81

Lesson 22: **Why Babies Are Cute** 85

Lesson 23: **Booker's Dream** 89

Lesson 24: **The Sport of Fencing** 93

Lesson 25: **Killer Whales** 97

Lesson 26: **The Star-Spangled Banner** 101

Lesson 27: **Ants for Dinner** 105

Lesson 28: **Earthquakes** 109

Lesson 29: **The Good Snake** 113

Lesson 30: **Those Miserable Allergies** 117

Lesson 31: **Four Marsupials** 121

Lesson 32: **Jumping Firefighters** 125

Lesson 33: **Just a Matter of Time** 129

Lesson 34: **Reading Between the Lines** 133

Lesson 35: **A Talented American** 137

Lesson 36: **Memory Tips** 141

Lesson 37: **Wordless Stories** 145

Lesson 38: **Graphically Speaking** . . . 149

Lesson 39: **Facts at a Glance** 153

Lesson 40: **An Organized View** 157

Lesson 41: **Let It Snow, Let It Snow, Let It Snow** 161

Lesson 42: **World Religions** 165

Lesson 43: **Finding Books at the Library** 169

Lesson 44: **Using the Card Catalog** 173

Lesson 45: **Trivia and More** 177

Lesson 46: **No Loss for Words** 181

Lesson 47: **Walter Hunt and the Safety Pin** 185

Lesson 48: **Special Aids in Dictionaries and Encyclopedias** 189

Lesson 49: **Order in the Court** 193

Lesson 50: **Feline Facts** 197

Lesson 51: **Cash or Charge** 201

Lesson 52: **Every Dog Should Own a Human** 205

Lesson 53: **Matters of Money** 209

Lesson 54: **It's Dabatable** 213

Lesson 55: **The Question Is** 217

Lesson 56: **Junk Food Junkie** 221

Mini-book: **Boss Cat** 225

Word Histories

Have you ever wondered why a word means what it means? Why do we call chocolate, lollipops, and jelly beans candy? Who gave a hammer its name? In this lesson, you will learn the history of some English words.

KEYS to Etymology

English words come from many languages.

LEARN   The study of the history of words is called *etymology*. Many words in the English language have been borrowed from other languages.

EXAMPLE

Word	Original Language	Original Meaning
alligator	Spanish	great lizard
bonus	Latin	good
chop suey	Chinese	odds and ends
democracy	Greek	rule of the people
iceberg	Dutch	ice mountain
kindergarten	German	children's garden

DIRECTIONS   Write a word from the list to complete each sentence.

1. The word for a dish made from several different foods came from the

   _____ language.

2. When you know that *berg* means *mountain,* you are speaking the language of the

   _____ people.

3. In German, the word *kinder* means _____

   and *garten* means _____ .

2 Practice With Etymology

DIRECTIONS Many English words came from Old English, French, Italian, Latin, and Greek. Spanish, Portuguese, Danish, Norwegian, Swedish, and other languages also contributed to the English language. Read about each borrowed word. Then answer the questions.

Curfew comes from a French word which means *to cover the fire*. In the Middle Ages, most buildings were made of wood and, therefore, burned easily. A bell was rung at sunset each night to notify people to extinguish the fires and candles in their homes.

Khaki, meaning *yellowish brown*, has come to be used to mean a heavy cotton yellowish-brown cloth often used to make uniforms. A *Hindi* word for *dust* or *dirt* gave the English language the word *khaki*.

A Greek word for *ship* gave the English language the words *nausea* meaning *seasickness* and *nautical* meaning *having to do with ships and sailing*. One who is nauseous feels about to vomit or feels that something is distasteful or disgusting.

Preposterous comes from a Turkish word meaning *empty* or *useless*. The word is a combination of the prefix *pre* meaning *before* and *post* meaning *after*. Germans referred to "putting the cart before the horse" as being ridiculous, which is the meaning of *preposterous*.

Metropolis is from two ancient Greek words meaning *mother* and *city*. A metropolis was the mother city, and it continues to mean the main city in an area today.

Courage was borrowed from a Latin word meaning *heart*. People who are courageous act from their hearts and aren't fearful in times of danger.

Chandelier comes from an old French word for a candle. Although early chandeliers held candles, today most chandeliers use electricity.

1. Which word might describe fabric or its color?

   _____

2. What language gave a word for a bad feeling in the stomach?

   _____

3. What word describes the quality the cowardly lion lacked in the movie "Wizard of Oz"?

   _____

4. What word tells when to be home at night?

   _____

5. What word describes an absolutely silly idea?

   _____

6. What language gave English the word for a light fixture?

   _____

7. What language gave English the word *metropolitan*?

   _____

3 Read and Apply

DIRECTIONS Read about the origins of some words about food.

Many foods which are considered "All-American" really have their origins in other countries. The hamburger and frankfurter, or hotdog, are German foods. The hamburger takes its name from the city of Hamburg, Germany, and frankfurters come from Frankfurt, Germany.

Credit for the popular dip or topping called *ketchup,* sometimes written *catsup,* is shared by the Chinese and Malaysians, who developed the sauce, and the Dutch who introduced it to England. The English are also credited, since they added tomatoes to the sauce to give it the color and taste we know today.

Speaking of tomatoes, the word for this popular juicy fruit came from Spanish, as did the word *potato.* Potatoes were discovered in the Andes Mountains of South America and introduced to Europeans by the Spanish. From Europe, potatoes found their way to Ireland, where they became an important

food. When the Irish traveled to the United States, they introduced this white vegetable with brown or red skin.

The Germans and Dutch introduced pretzels and cookies to Americans. They also took dumplings, noodles, strudels, and their dark bread, called pumpernickel, to America.

Of course, the Italians are credited with the introduction of pizza and other popular foods like macaroni, ravioli, salami, spumoni ice cream, and broccoli.

The word *candy* comes from Sanskrit, an ancient language of India. Marshmallows were eaten in Italy over 2,000 years ago, while chocolate is a gift from the Aztec Indians who lived in Mexico over 500 years ago. Chocolate marshmallow candy is a product of three different nationalities.

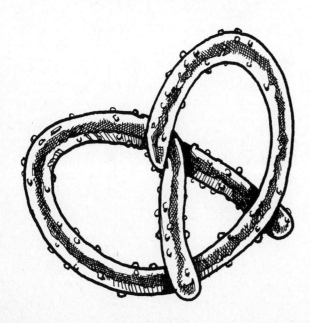

DIRECTIONS Use the article you just read and the clues provided to complete the puzzle below. Then read down the shaded boxes and write the hidden message to answer question 11.

1. The city where hamburgers originated.
2. As American as _____ pie.
3. A gift from Italy that goes well with cheese.
4. A vegetable with an Italian name.
5. A dark bread from Germany.
6. A German dessert made with fruit or cheese and rolled up in a thin sheet of dough before being baked.

7. _____ and meatballs.
8. It was brought to Europe where the English added tomatoes.
9. A thin roll of dough baked in the form of a loose knot on a stick and sometimes salted on the outside.
10. An Italian ice cream.
11. Fast-Foods

_____

REMEMBER Many English words originated elsewhere.

4

Strictly American

Why is someone with power sometimes called a bigwig? Where did a parka get its name? When is a snowstorm a blizzard? In this lesson, you'll learn about some words whose origins are strictly American.

KEYS to Etymology

Every word in the English language came from somewhere.

LEARN *Etymology* is the study of the origin of words. English words come from a variety of sources. Although many words come from the languages of other countries, there are other words whose origins are strictly American.

EXAMPLE It was fashionable in the early days of Williamsburg, Virginia for the men to wear powdered wigs. These wigs came in different lengths and styles. The longer, more elaborate wigs were also the most expensive. Wealthy town leaders and merchants were the only ones who could afford the larger wigs. The ordinary citizens of the town called these men *bigwigs*.

DIRECTIONS Read about the American origin of a word. Then write the word that will complete the paragraph.

A. The first car was called a horseless carriage because it looked like the carriages that were pulled by horses. Later, these vehicles were referred to as being "automatically mobile," meaning they could move by their own power. Today, a four-wheeled, land vehicle with an engine and room for a driver and passenger is called a/an

_____

DIRECTIONS   Read the words in the box. Then read each sentence. Write a word from the box to complete each sentence.

bumpers	freeways
electrician	everglades
kidnap	skunk
windshield	boxcars
parka	

1. As trains became bigger and more powerful, large box-like containers were made. These containers on wheels are called

   _____ .

2. The _____ , a hooded coat, was invented in Alaska as a protection from the wind and cold.

3. Benjamin Franklin invented the word

   _____

   to describe someone who was interested in working with electricity.

4. Manufacturers add protective pieces to the front and back of an automobile to absorb shock in the event of a collision. These pieces are called

   _____ .

5. The automobile brought the need for wide, four-lane highways called

   _____

   for faster travel from city to city.

6. The glass shield that kept the wind from blowing on the driver and passengers of newly-developed automobiles was called a

   _____ .

7. Two slang words, *kid,* meaning *young child,* and *nap,* meaning *to steal,* form

   _____

   which means *to steal people away.*

8. When Florida became part of the United States, the word

   _____

   was invented to describe the green, lush swamp there.

9. A small, black and white animal which sometimes gave off a foul-smelling odor was named

   _____

   by the American Indian.

Read and Apply

Read about the origin of a word for a blinding snowstorm.

There is some disagreement among etymologists about the origin of the word *blizzard*. Most agree that the word as we know it today was first used in the United States in the latter part of the 1800s. Some researchers credit a New York newspaper editor with the first use of the word in 1881 to describe severe winter weather in the Northeast. Others claim an editor in Iowa first used the term to describe a fierce snowstorm in 1870.

Regardless of which editor deserves credit, the word was used to describe the same kind of event. A blizzard meant, and still does, a violent snowstorm. The word *blizzard* had other meanings prior to the late 1800s. In 1770, a blizzard was a heavy rain. Davy Crockett is said to have used the term to mean the heavy round of shots fired at a deer. Then there was the blizzard that referred to the final knockout punch delivered by a prizefighter. Other references are made to the word's relationship to the German word *blitz* which means *lightning*.

According to the U.S. Weather Bureau, an official blizzard must have winds of 40 miles or more per hour, temperatures near zero, and lots of fine, swirling snow. For many years, the record blizzard in the United States was in New York City in 1888. Many weather watchers claim that the 1888 blizzard was worse than modern blizzards, because in those days there were no fast methods of clearing the snow. In 1946, almost 26 inches of snow fell on New York City in less than 24 hours. The Weather Bureau did not call the snowstorm a blizzard, however, since the winds and temperatures were not severe enough.

The amount of snowfall in a blizzard may not tell the true story of a blizzard. Two feet of snow can seem like much more, especially when high winds cause snowdrifts ten or twenty feet high.

1. What official group decides when a snowstorm can be called a blizzard?

   _____

   _____

2. What three things must be evident for a storm to be considered an official blizzard?

   a. _____

   _____

   _____

   b. _____

   _____

   _____

   c. _____

   _____

   _____

3. Why might it be difficult to determine exact facts about a word's origin?

   a. Nobody is interested enough to search for origins of words.

   b. The word isn't used enough today.

   c. Records are not available, or they give differing stories.

   d. Records are all destroyed, and etymologists have to make up stories.

4. What word is used for snow that's piled up by a blowing wind?

   _____

5. List three uses for the word *blizzard* prior to its use to describe a snowstorm.

   a. _____

   _____

   b. _____

   _____

   _____

   c. _____

   _____

6. Why might some say that New York City's blizzard of 1888 was the worst ever in the U.S.?

   a. People today remember very well how they had to shovel the snow.

   b. There weren't any fast methods of clearing the snow then.

   c. There were more inches of snow than any storm since then.

   d. The storm caused most people to be snowbound.

REMEMBER Many English words were coined in the United States.

What's the Forecast?

Lesson 3

How can there be a downpour today when last weekend's forecast called for sunshine all week? In this lesson, you'll read about weather as you learn about special words for special topics.

 1 KEYS to Content Words

Every subject area has its own special words.

LEARN   There are special words for every subject. Specific topics in each of the subject areas also have their own *content words*. Content words are usually the most important words in a sentence.

EXAMPLE   Knowing the meanings of special content words helps you get the most meaning from this sentence:

The forecast is for heavy precipitation.

Forecast means to predict what will happen, and *precipitation* refers to the amount of rain or snow that falls from the air.

DIRECTIONS   Read the paragraph. Write a word or phrase from the paragraph beside its description.

When atmospheric conditions are just right, two destructive types of weather may occur. A tornado is a high, narrow, whirling column of air. It is often seen as a funnel-shaped cloud. Drastic pressure changes in the funnel of a tornado usually cause everything in a tornado's path to be destroyed. A hurricane is a strong windstorm where the wind blows in a large circle at over 70 mph. Hurricanes usually develop in the Gulf of Mexico or the Atlantic Ocean.

1. These cause a tornado to do much damage. _____

2. These develop over water. _____

Content Words **9**

DIRECTIONS It is often helpful to use the context, or the other words around a word, to get the meaning of a content word. Read each definition of a weather word. Then read each sentence. Write the letter of the definition that best describes the underlined word or phrase.

a. the most common type of storm that brings rain, thunder, and lightning

b. a prediction about the weather over the next 18 to 36 hours

c. most violent of all storms with winds swirling in a funnel

d. person who studies weather and makes forecasts

e. a large storm that forms over the ocean but weakens when it reaches land

f. a term used to describe air that's full of water vapor when humidity is high

g. prediction about the weather over the next 5 days, 6 to 10 days, or 30 days

h. dampness or amount of water vapor in the air

i. the air that surrounds the earth

j. the force of the atmosphere pushing on the earth

_____ 1. The short-range forecast suggests that our plans for tomorrow will have to be postponed.

_____ 2. The hurricane caused extensive flooding in Florida and the Carolinas.

_____ 3. About 50,000 thunderstorms occur in the world each day.

_____ 4. Tornadoes are most common in the Midwestern and Southern regions of the United States.

_____ 5. Since warm air weighs less than cool air, warm air forms a low air pressure area, while cool air forms a high-pressure area.

_____ 6. All weather develops in the atmosphere where water vapor and particles of dust are mixed.

_____ 7. Meteorologists prepare weather maps and then analyze them to make predictions.

_____ 8. When the humidity is high, the air is holding all the moisture possible.

_____ 9. Extended forecasts are updated daily, three times a week, or twice a month and are likely to be less accurate than forecasts over a shorter time period.

_____ 10. When humidity is high, we say that the air is saturated.

DIRECTIONS   As you read the article on rain, think about the meanings of the under-lined words.

A sudden <u>downpour</u> that forces a baseball game to be canceled also fills lakes and streams where wildlife live. The continuous <u>drizzle</u> that ruins a day at the beach also waters farmers' crops. We may complain, but most living things depend on rain for survival.

Rain may fall to earth in different ways, but the manner in which it begins to form is the same. Every day, the sun's heat <u>evaporates</u> billions of gallons of water from wet places on the earth. This water turns into a gas called <u>water vapor</u>. As the water vapor rises higher and higher, it grows cool. When it gets cool enough, the invisible water vapor <u>condenses</u> into very small round <u>spheres</u> of water. Then, these tiny <u>droplets</u> form around small solid <u>particles</u> already in the air.

When you look at a cloud in the sky, you are looking at millions and millions of tiny droplets. If a cloud formed over the sea, the droplets <u>initially</u> began to grow on tiny grains of salt. If a cloud was formed by winds blowing over land, the cloud droplets first formed around bits of dust. Although all rain begins as cloud droplets, the type of rain that finally falls to earth depends on what happens after the droplets are formed.

Drizzle begins in a cloud when the temperature is above freezing. Each water droplet continues to grow as more water condenses into it from the air. Then droplets of different sizes <u>collide</u> and <u>merge</u> together into larger droplets. As the droplets grow and grow, they become too heavy to float in the air. Eventually, these droplets fall out of the cloud as soft rain. However, it takes a long time for these tiny droplets to grow big enough to overcome the air that supports them. Sometimes the whole cloud evaporates and disappears before this happens, so we get very little rain this way.

Most rain starts in thick, cold clouds that contain both water droplets and <u>ice crystals</u>. When clouds become thick, the temperature at the top of the clouds is well below freezing. At these low temperatures, the water droplets freeze and turn into ice crystals. These ice crystals grow quickly by combining with one another. As they fall down into the thick cloud, these larger crystals may reach a level where the temperature is above freezing. When this happens, the big ice crystals melt and change into water droplets. These descend from the cloud as large raindrops, and a shower or thunderstorm occurs.

<u>Precipitation</u> continues until all the larger droplets in the cloud have fallen. The rain gives people, plants, and animals a fresh source of water. If a cloud loses all the water it contains and does not receive a new supply of moisture from the air, it will slowly disappear.

DIRECTIONS Read each sentence. Write an underlined word from the article you just read to complete the sentence.

1. Clouds are made up of very small spheres of water called

   _____ .

2. _____ is another word for a soft rain.

3. A basketball and a globe are examples of things that are the shape of a

   _____ .

4. *Combine* and *blend* are words that mean the same as

   _____ .

5. Since water vapor is a gas that cannot be seen, you could say it is

   _____ .

6. Rain, sleet, and hail are types of

   _____ .

7. Another word that means "dries up" is

   _____ .

8. When a gas, like water vapor, changes to a liquid, like water droplets, it

   _____ .

9. If you bump into something, you

   _____

   with it.

10. A heavy rain is often called a

    _____ .

11. Clouds that produce rain usually contain water droplets and

    _____ .

12. When water evaporates, it becomes

    _____ .

REMEMBER Special subjects have special content words.

When the Earth Quakes

Have you noticed how every subject in school seems to have its own special vocabulary? Special words pop up in your science book, but you rarely see those words in your math book or social studies books. In this lesson, you will learn about special vocabularies. You'll read about violent shaking of the earth.

 ## KEYS to Content Words

Some words are unique to each special subject.

LEARN Content words are words with specific meanings for a particular subject area. To understand a subject, you need to master the special words, terms, and expressions from that subject.

DIRECTIONS Read the paragraph. Then read each definition and circle the word in the paragraph. Write the word on the line.

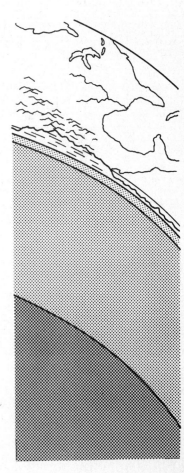

Planet earth is shaped like a three-layered ball. If you were to cut out a cross-section of earth, you would see a series of circles. The outside layer or shell-like material is called the crust. Its thickness varies from 5 to 40 miles. Below the crust is an even thicker layer called the mantle, which is about 1,800 miles deep. At the center of the earth is the deepest layer, the core. The core is about 2,100 miles thick. Together, these three layers make up our earth.

1. Earth's middle layer _____

2. Earth's outside layer _____

3. Center of Earth _____

DIRECTIONS Read each sentence and the definition below it. Underline the content word in the sentence that matches the definition.

1. Most landslides occur along mountainsides and other steep-sided hills.
   Definition: *mass movement of large amounts of soil and rock*

2. A volcanic eruption causes changes in the earth's crust.
   Definition: *a bursting or throwing forth*

3. The earth's crust is continually changing because of erosion by wind, water, and glaciers.
   Definition: *movement of soil and other materials from high places to low places*

4. The magnitude of an earthquake is measured on a scale of 1 to 10.
   Definition: *strength or greatness*

5. When the force of the earth's rocks pressing against each other becomes too great, a rupture causes an earthquake.
   Definition: *a break*

6. Nearly all the world's major earthquakes occur in one of two areas known as the circum-Pacific belt and the Alpine belt.
   Definition: *most important*

7. Scientists hope to use the history of previous earthquakes to predict future quakes.
   Definition: *earlier or that which comes before*

8. Although the focus of most earthquakes is 25 miles or less below the earth's surface, a few earthquakes happen at the surface or as far as 400 miles below the surface.
   Definition: *a specific point where movement begins*

Think about the meanings of the content words as you read about earthquakes.

The earth is a living, changing planet. Because of its great inner heat and the weight of rocks pressing on other rocks, many things are happening. Inside the mantle and crust, huge rocks are constantly being pulled, pushed, twisted, squeezed, and strained. Sometimes, rock is under so much strain that it suddenly slips or breaks. When this happens, there is a jolting movement. The shifting or breaking rock jolts all the rock around it. It is this movement you feel in an earthquake.

To see what happens when rock inside the earth suddenly moves, try this: Fill a deep basin with water. Pretend the water is inside the earth. Tie a string to a small rock. Lower the rock to the bottom of the basin. When the water is completely still, jerk the rock up suddenly. What happens? Waves are formed by the rock's sudden movement. These waves ripple the surface of the water in bigger and bigger circles.

Waves caused by earthquakes are called seismic waves. Usually, you can't see them, but you can feel them. The place deep in the earth where the rock first shifts or breaks is called the focus of the quake. The epicenter of the quake is where the waves reach the surface of the earth, straight above the focus.

Like giant pushing hands, seismic waves travel outward from the focus of an earthquake in circles that steadily

increase in size. The waves can be traced by what they do to the rock they go through, and by the damage they cause on the surface of the earth. Seismic waves are what cause the violent shaking in an earthquake.

The earth shakes every thirty seconds. Some areas of the world experience up to sixty mini-earthquakes in one day's time. Most are too small to feel, but scientists know they have occurred. Scientists call a series of earthquakes a swarm.

Earthquake scientists use seismographs to measure quakes. Seismographs are very sensitive electrical instruments that detect and record the earth's movements. The instrument is shaped like a drum and has paper stretched across it. A thin pen hangs just above the paper. Whenever the earth shakes, the pen records the movement on the drum's paper. The record that is made is called a seismogram.

Seismograms taken in offices nearest the epicenter of the earthquake record the strongest vibrations, or seismic waves. The seismogram tells earthquake scientists, called seismologists, when the quake occurred, where the epicenter is located, and the depth of the focus.

Seismologists study the records to determine the severity of a quake. They use a scale of numbers, called the Richter scale, to measure the strength or amount of energy released by earthquakes. The Richter scale was developed by Dr. Charles F. Richter. It goes from a low of 1 to a high of 10. If a quake measures 2 on the Richter scale, people may feel a slight tremor, or shake, of the earth. Quakes that measure 5 will cause damage to property. Serious damage is caused by earthquakes measuring 7 and above. These are major disasters. The strongest earthquake ever measured rated 8.9 on the Richter scale.

DIRECTIONS Circle the letter of the answer that defines each word as used in the article above.

1. A seismologist is a
   a. chart of the earth's movements.
   b. person who studies quake records.
   c. person who studies peoples' sizes.

2. A swarm is
   a. many quakes in a series.
   b. a 30-second shake.
   c. a collection of bees.

3. A seismograph is
   a. a paper showing waves of the sea.
   b. a chart of epicenters.
   c. an instrument for measuring quakes.

4. A tremor is a
   a. shaking in the earth's layers.
   b. number on the Richter scale.
   c. muscle spasm.

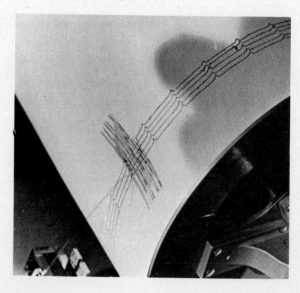

REMEMBER All subjects have special vocabularies.

Bridging the Gap

Long ago, people found that if they wanted to move around on the earth, they needed to find ways to get across water and other gaps between stretches of land. In this lesson, you'll read about ways that gaps are bridged. You'll also learn about words whose meanings are similar.

1 KEYS to Synonyms

Many words mean almost the same thing.

LEARN Words with the same or similar meanings are called *synonyms*. Some words have several synonyms that can be used interchangeably. Other synonyms give a more precise description or present a picture that is a bit different. Synonyms allow us to choose the most precise word to describe something.

EXAMPLE Covered bridges are odd today.
Covered bridges are unusual today.

Although *odd* and *unusual* have similar meanings, it is more correct to say that covered bridges are unusual today, since there are few of them.

DIRECTIONS Circle the synonym in parentheses that goes best with the other words in the sentence.

1. We were (pleased / thrilled) when the bridge was completed and we no longer had to detour that twenty miles.

2. Some bridges are (suspended / held) by cables that are strung between towers.

3. The bridge's birthday celebration was (colorful / spectacular) with many well-planned festivities for masses of people.

② Practice With Synonyms

DIRECTIONS Read the list of words. Then read each sentence. Write a synonym from the list on the line after each word in parentheses.

unmoving	bendable	undependable	strengthened
stretching	repair	lasting	create
naturally	walkers	limited	

1. Suspension bridges must withstand the (tension) _____ caused by the pulling of the cables.

2. Steel is used in bridge construction because it is strong and (durable)

   _____ .

3. Cast iron, or iron poured into molds to harden in particular shapes, was used earlier in the construction of arch bridges only, since it was not (flexible)

   _____ and, therefore, most (unreliable) _____ .

4. The first iron bridge still stands today in Coalbrookdale, England, but travel is (restricted) _____ to (pedestrians) _____ and bicycles.

5. Although concrete is (inherently) _____ strong, it is (reinforced) _____ with steel for use in building bridges.

6. An advantage of using concrete in bridge construction is that it has many uses and requires little (maintenance) _____ .

7. Many viaducts, or bridges over land or highways, (form) _____ short tunnels.

8. Although most bridges are (stationary) _____ , drawbridges are movable to allow the passage of ships beneath them.

DIRECTIONS Read about the types of bridge construction.

All bridges are constructed for a similar purpose—to connect two areas that are separated by a barrier. Usually, the barrier is water or a canyon, although bridges are also erected to go over buildings and flat land.

Bridge construction requires much planning and time. Designers and engineers must know the depth and width of the barrier, what types of vehicles will travel on the bridge, and the quality of the land on both sides and the bottom of the water or canyon. If a bridge is to be erected over water, specialists must also determine whether large ships will be traversing the water beneath the structure. If the bridge must accommodate water travel beneath it, it must be a sufficient height above the water, or a drawbridge must be planned to allow ships to pass through.

Bridge designers analyze all the criteria to make two crucial decisions—the kind of bridge construction that best suits the specific needs of the site and the materials that will be used. A combination of stone, concrete, and steel is usually the choice of building materials, since a bridge must withstand years of wear from vehicle use, weather elements, and any future floods or collisions such as those caused by shipping accidents.

There are several basic types of bridge construction. A bridge may be a combination of the three types. A beam bridge, the most basic type, is best compared to a log stretched across a stream. With the addition of numerous supports, though, beam bridges can span great distances. Because they are usually low with a minimum of distance between their supports, beam bridges are impractical in situations requiring clearance for large vessels. Truss bridges are beam-type bridges which gain their rigidity from triangular supports.

A cantilever bridge, another beam-type structure, is usually constructed in two sections which resemble diving boards extending from opposite banks. A special truss connecting the two sections acts as an expansion joint which provides for the natural expansion and contraction that occur when the temperature changes.

Some of the earliest arch-type bridges, such as the Ponte Sant'Angelo, erected over the Tiber River in Rome in 134 A.D., still exist. Although such bridges were appropriately named for their arch-like openings that provided support and allowed flooding waters to pass through, today's arch bridges generally curve in from the ends for a rainbow effect. The arch form that gives the bridge its strength, is supported by scaffolding until the bridge is completed.

In 1883, the Brooklyn Bridge on Manhattan Island made its debut and set a world record as the longest suspension bridge. Other bridges have exceeded the record since, with the Golden Gate Bridge over San Francisco Bay and the Verrazano–Narrows Bridge over the New York harbor nearly tripling it. Suspension bridges, structures supported between towers by cables, are favored for spanning navigable waterways, since they can stretch over greater distances and soar the highest above the water.

DIRECTIONS Match each numbered word with its synonym from the list at the right. Write the letter on the line.

_____ 1. expansion   **a.** built

_____ 2. appropriately   **b.** rightly

_____ 3. contraction   **c.** opening

_____ 4. debut   **d.** enough

_____ 5. analyze   **e.** enlarging

_____ 6. minimum   **f.** shrinking

_____ 7. rigidity   **g.** allow

_____ 8. erected   **h.** study

_____ 9. crucial   **i.** necessary

_____ 10. sufficient   **j.** useless

_____ 11. accommodate   **k.** least

_____ 12. clearance   **l.** traveling

_____ 13. impractical   **m.** stiffness

_____ 14. traversing   **n.** space

REMEMBER Some words have several different synonyms.

Fortress Or Luxury?

Why would anyone build a castle? In this lesson, you'll read about why castles were built long ago and why a castle was built during the twentieth century. You'll learn about words with opposite meanings.

 1 **KEYS to Antonyms**

Words with opposite meanings are antonyms.

LEARN Words with opposite meanings are called *antonyms*. When antonyms are substituted for words in a sentence, the whole meaning changes.

DIRECTIONS Read each sentence. Find the antonym of the underlined word in the word box. Write it on the line.

simple	unprotected	destruction	loosely

1. The <u>construction</u> of castles in the Middle Ages was for protection during wars.

   _____

2. People from all around flocked to the <u>fortified</u> castles at the first sign of war.

   _____

3. Laws were <u>strictly</u> enforced inside the castle walls.

   _____

4. People in modern times have erected <u>luxurious</u> castles to house collections of art and other rare pieces.

   _____

2 Practice With Antonyms

DIRECTIONS Read each sentence. Then write each underlined word on the line before its antonym and definition below.

1. When a castle was taken by the enemy, all the lands around it became the property of the <u>victor</u>.

2. Castles were a <u>prominent</u> part of life in the Middle Ages.

3. Castles erected on flat land had moats around them to discourage <u>offensive</u> attacks.

4. During the Middle Ages, a lord designed and built his castle to show his power and <u>dignity</u>.

5. Medieval castles had to be <u>massive</u>, since a whole army would <u>live there</u> during the height of a battle.

6. A narrow balcony just above a castle's entrance <u>afforded</u> defenders a place from <u>which</u> to <u>hurl</u> boiling oil or tar on attackers.

7. The improvement of weapons was <u>partially</u> responsible for the end of <u>castle life</u>.

8. The appearance of some castles has changed, since <u>restorations</u> have not always been in <u>keeping</u> with the original look.

9. Since the vassals were defenseless without the protection of the lords, they were totally <u>obedient</u>.

10. Ordinary men found themselves fighting armored soldiers, while they were <u>scantily</u> dressed in their few bits of <u>clothing</u>.

11. During peaceful times, the most important event in a castle was the banquet when people would feast <u>endlessly</u>.

_____ **a.** miniscule—extremely small

_____ **b.** profusely—greatly

_____ **c.** oppressed—those who are crushed by authority

_____ **d.** briefly—for a short time

_____ **e.** rebellious—going against the rules

_____ **f.** minor—a small part

_____ **g.** dishonor—lack of worth or honor

_____ **h.** demolitions—acts of tearing down or destroying

_____ **i.** entirely—all or totally

_____ **j.** defensive—protecting

_____ **k.** denied—not allowed

3 Read and Apply

DIRECTIONS Read about a castle built long after the Middle Ages for far different purposes.

In contrast to castles built for protection in the Middle Ages, some modern castles have been built primarily for leisure purposes. One of these is a major tourist attraction today.

William Randolph Hearst, a wealthy man and a collector of art objects, had a castle built on his late father's 240,000 acre estate on California's coastline. Located near the town of San Simeon, Hearst Castle sits on top of a small mountain. Hearst, owner and publisher of a large newspaper, wanted to have a place to entertain guests. He also desired an appropriate setting for his vast collection of art and antique furniture which was at one time considered to be the largest and most valuable collection ever privately owned by one person.

Construction, which began in 1919, continued for more than thirty years. Elaborate gardens, terraces, and pools decorate the castle on the 123-acre hilltop. Three grand cottages, each containing from ten to eighteen rooms, stand around the castle. One cottage faces the ocean, one overlooks the Santa Lucia Mountains, and the third cottage faces west to take advantage of the beautiful sunsets. The castle itself contains over 100 rooms including numerous bedrooms, sitting rooms, a private theater, an indoor pool, a library with over 5,000 rare books, and several game and entertainment rooms.

Tourists who visit the Hearst Castle ride a bus up the treacherous mountainside. En route to the castle, they occasionally spot a relative of the more than 100 species of wild animals once housed on 2,000 acres set aside as a zoo. Hearst's wild animals also represented a world-renowned record for a privately-owned collection.

Think about how each word was used in the article you just read. Match the word with its antonym from the list at the right. Write the letter on the line.

_____ 1. late   **a.** unknown

_____ 2. major   **b.** always

_____ 3. vast   **c.** safe

_____ 4. appropriate   **d.** worthless

_____ 5. occasionally   **e.** unsuitable

_____ 6. privately   **f.** living

_____ 7. elaborate   **g.** small

_____ 8. wealthy   **h.** simple

_____ 9. numerous   **i.** few

_____ 10. renowned   **j.** modern

_____ 11. valuable   **k.** work

_____ 12. treacherous   **l.** minor

_____ 13. antique   **m.** publicly

_____ 14. leisure   **n.** poor

DIRECTIONS Read each sentence. Find and circle a word in the sentence that is an antonym for the underlined word.

1. Women in medieval times had few pastimes, while men's activities were plentiful.

2. The kings and lords were wealthy, while the serfs were indigent.

3. Kings in the Middle Ages rewarded their lords for bravery but condemned them for disobedience.

4. Lords found fighting exciting partly because their lives were so boring during peacetime.

5. The vassals were made to feel inferior to the noblemen.

6. In order for kings to rule their vast lands, they had to have lords defend small areas.

7. The majestic castle of a nobleman was a sharp contrast to the measly homes of ordinary people, or peasants.

8. Defenders of a castle initially fought outside the castle, but finally, as a last resort, they'd retreat inside the walls.

REMEMBER Antonyms have opposite meanings.

Fads and Fashion

Did you ever hear an older person say, "Those clothes look just like the ones we wore a long time ago"? In this lesson, you'll read about fads and fashions. You'll learn about words that sound alike but are very different.

1 KEYS to Homonyms

Words may sound alike but have different meanings.

LEARN   *Homonyms* are words that sound alike but have different spellings and meanings. The spelling of the word and the rest of the words in a sentence tell you which meaning was used.

EXAMPLE   He *bowled* in special shoes and comfortable *clothes*.

I had to *close* my eyes at the *bold* colors.

The words *bowled* and *bold* sound alike but are spelled differently. *Bowled* means *played the game of bowling*, while *bold* means *daring*. *Close* and *clothes* are also homonyms.

DIRECTIONS   Circle the homonyms in each sentence.

1. All the bride's attendants were in attendance at the rehearsal.

2. No cars were in sight yet at the race site.

3. My guest arrived before I had guessed she would.

4. The designer showed disgust when the fashion editors discussed his rival's work.

2 Practice With Homonyms

DIRECTIONS Read the sentence. Choose the word whose definition helps the sentence make sense. Write the word on the line.

1. Most new fashions are _____ on previous styles.
    baste—to sew a temporary seam with large stitches
    based—patterned after

2. Fashion designers rename and slightly _____ old styles for new looks.
    alter—change
    altar—a high place used in religious ceremonies

3. One can often look back in history for similar versions of _____ fashions and fads.
    currant—a small, sweet black raisin
    current—of the present time

4. The _____ skirt of the 1850s returned in the 1950s.
    whoop—a cry of excitement
    hoop—a hollow circular piece

5. The clam-digger pants of the 1980s were _____ in the 1950s, but they were called pedal-pushers.
    worn—put on to wear
    warn—to tell of danger

6. A stretchy _____ worn around the head is a popular piece of equipment for runners.
    banned—forbidden
    band—a narrow piece of fabric or other material

7. Young people are often _____ that the latest fad has never been seen before, although older people may say differently.
    confident—sure
    confidant—a close, trusted friend

8. Some people have the _____ and the storage space to save out-of-style clothes in hope the fashions will return.
    patients—people under a doctor's care
    patience—ability to wait

Read and Apply

Look for words that are part of a homonym pair as you read about fads and fashion.

When many people do a similar thing at the same time, their behavior is in fashion. Although the word *fashion* generally refers to clothing styles, it is also used to describe other trends. A particular form of music, a sports activity, use of specific words, and hair styles are examples of other ideas that show fashion.

Fashions are usually popular for a period of time, and then become *old-fashioned* as they're replaced by new ideas. Most changes in fashion are minor, since people don't easily accept extreme changes. Therefore, a new fashion is often similar to an old one.

Sometimes there are drastic changes in fashion, though. *Fads* are fashions that are "here today and gone tomorrow." Fads are often adopted by particular groups, but not by the majority of people. The hula hoop and the skateboard were fads in the 1950s, as was the flat-top hairstyle for men and boys.

Before the 1300s, clothing fashions did not change drastically. As kings and lords of the Middle Ages began to lose their power, however, they chose to dress in elaborate clothing in order to appear more distinguished than the common people. Major inventions also contributed to fashion changes. Mass-production of clothes in the 1800s lowered clothing costs and made items available in large quantities. People's activities also influenced fashion, as participation in sports suggested special outfits. When long-distance travel was made easier by the invention of airplanes, styles of dress were shared in different lands, and new fashions appeared.

Fashion trends are sometimes repeated in cycles. Some 1950s clothing, hairstyles, and toys, for example, returned in the 1980s. Women of the 1940s wore wide-legged pants similar to the bell-bottoms of the 1960s. The hula hoop had a brief return in the 1970s, and skateboarding attracted a sizeable following of young people in the 1980s.

Sometimes a fashion is so popular it becomes a custom as it remains and is passed down from generation to generation. In the 1800s, long trousers replaced the knee-length breeches worn by men in Europe and the United

States. Although colors and shapes of pants have changed over the years, the long pants have become customary male attire.

Elvis Presley and his rock-and-roll music were initially considered a fad in the 1950s. People were sure the music and the musician would be "out of style" soon. The continued popularity of Rock-and-Roll and the legendary status of Elvis Presley have proven that some fads also become customs.

DIRECTIONS Find a word in the article you just read to answer each question. Write the word on the line. What is the homonym for:

1. *breaches* that tells a style of pants?

_____

2. *thyme* that is measured in minutes, hours, etc.?

_____

3. *they're* that shows ownership?

_____

4. *maid* that is a form of the word *make?*

_____

5. *stiles* that describes forms of fashion?

_____

6. *close* that names what people wear?

_____

7. *won* that is a number?

_____

8. *hare* that covers people's heads?

_____

9. *whoop* that describes a hollow circular piece?

_____

10. *war* that is a form of *wear?*

_____

11. *there* that is a contraction?

_____

12. *buoys* that means young males?

_____

13. *mail* that means the opposite of *female?*

_____

14. *moor* that means *a greater amount?*

_____

15. *past* that means *went by?*

_____

16. *sew* that means *therefore* or *extreme?*

_____

17. *miner* that means *small* or *to a lesser degree?*

_____

REMEMBER Check spelling and meaning when two words sound alike.

Let the Show Begin

Dim the lights! Strike up the band! Shine the spotlights! "Ladies and gentlemen, boys and girls! Welcome to the most daring, wonderful, spectacular, sensational, amazing show ever performed!"

In this lesson, you'll read about the circus as you learn a way to figure out the meanings of unfamiliar words.

 ## 1 KEYS to Context Clues

Words work together to give meaning.

LEARN *Context* is a group of words that go together for meaning. When you don't know the meaning of one of those words, you can get help by reading the rest of the words.

EXAMPLE Circus performances *entice* people of all ages.

You can tell from the context that the word *entice* must mean *attract*.

DIRECTIONS Read each sentence. Circle the letter of the meaning that would make sense if it were substituted for the underlined word.

1. Many different circuses toured all over the United States in the 1880s and 1890s.

   a. shouted **b.** traveled **c.** guessed

2. After World War I and the depression, many circus families deserted their native countries to go to the United States to perform.

   a. enjoyed **b.** stayed in **c.** left

2 Practice With Context

DIRECTIONS Use context to find the meaning of each underlined word. Write the meaning on the line.

1. Circuses in the United States were initially only on the East Coast, since few people had ventured farther west then.

   Initially means _____

   _____ .

   Ventured means _____

   _____ .

2. The majority of circus aerialists have come from the United States, possibly because there are many large barns in rural areas that allowed space for trapeze practice.

   Majority means _____

   _____ .

   Rural means _____

   _____ .

3. The first circus families had specialties, with each family known for one particular act.

   Specialties means_____

   _____ .

4. Circus elephants were utilized for more than performing when they pushed and pulled circus wagons out of mud on the unpaved roads.

   Utilized means _____

   _____ .

5. In Roman days, gladiators and a variety of other acts, like wild animals and fire eaters were popular entertainment.

   Variety means _____

   _____ .

6. Great stadiums were built in Roman times to accommodate gladiator shows and other forms of entertainment.

   Accommodate means _____

   _____ .

7. As people who settled farther and farther west yearned for circus entertainment, performers began to travel west in wagons.

   Yearned means _____

   _____ .

Read and Apply

Read about some circus acts and the invention of pink lemonade.

What is a circus without a trapeze act? The first aerialist was Marguerite Lalanne, a French woman whose stage name was Madame Saqui. Marguerite began training for rope walking at a very young age. In 1816, she performed a midnight aerial act on a rope strung high above a crowd of thousands of people. Dressed in a glittering dress, Madame Saqui danced on the rope as brilliant fireworks sparkled around her.

One of the most famous aerialists to perform on the trapeze was Alfredo Codona of Mexico. In 1930, at the Chicago Coliseum, he achieved something the circus world thought to be impossible—the triple somersault. After three years of rehearsing, Codona finally succeeded in demonstrating this daring, dangerous feat.

Perhaps the most well-known aerialists of the modern day circus are the Wallendas. This family of aerialists had a dispute with their circus owner until he finally allowed them to perfect an aerial act on a suspended wire 100 feet in the air. The climax of their act was the formation of a human pyramid with all seven of the Wallendas on the wire at once.

Watching an aerialist high in the air can be hard on the neck, just as munching on popcorn and peanuts can cause real thirst. A popular beverage for the circus crowd is pink lemonade, which tastes the same as yellow lemonade, but seems special because of its color. Legend says a former clown can be credited with the discovery of pink lemonade.

For more than a generation in the old-time wagon shows, pink lemonade was the favorite beverage of summertime circus-goers who needed to wash down their peanuts and popcorn. But why pink?

There was once an ex-clown named Pete Conklin who discovered that it was more profitable to make lemonade and sell it to the sweltering customers than to cavort around the ring in Joey make-

up. No lemon ever found its way into his lemonade. He concocted it from tartaric acid, sugar, and a large chunk of ice to keep it cool.

One simmering afternoon in a small Southern town Pete found business so thriving that his supply ran out. He scurried into the back yard to get more water, but all he could find was a washtub in which a lady acrobat had just rinsed out her pretty pink tights. He quickly mixed in his ingredients and set up for business again. The customers found the color of the lemonade so pleasingly different that thereafter Pete always added a harmless vegetable coloring to his product. Lemonade vendors in other shows followed suit, and "pink lemonade" became as much a part of the circus world as peanuts or elephants.

DIRECTIONS Use the underlined words to help you answer the questions.

1. Which words suggest that Pete Conklin sold pink lemonade in the hot summer months?

   _____

   _____

2. What two words describe how Pete moved?

   _____

   _____

3. What word is another name for a Joey?

   _____

4. Which gave Pete Conklin the better income, being a Joey or being a vendor?

   _____

5. Which word describes a business that makes money?

   _____

6. What beverage did circus-goers use to wash down peanuts and popcorn?

   _____

7. What flavor does tartaric acid add to a beverage?

   _____

8. Which word shows that Pete had a lot of business the day his lemonade supply ran out?

   _____

9. Which word means that Conklin combined things to make a beverage?

   _____

10. What ingredients did Pete use to make "pink lemonade"?

   _____

   _____

REMEMBER Read all the words to figure out an unknown word.

Humble Papa Haydn

The English language contains over one million words. Because the language contains so many words, we cannot know all those words and their meanings. In this lesson, you will learn to use context clues to understand unfamiliar words. You'll read about a famous composer.

1 KEYS to Context Clues

Words around an unknown word can give you its meaning.

LEARN It is easier to understand a word's meaning in a sentence because all the other words around the unfamiliar word will help you. The whole statement or situation in which a word is used is called *context*. Good use of context clues will help you figure out the meaning of a word without the help of a dictionary.

EXAMPLE My baby brother is at an obstinate stage where he says "no" to everything.

By using the context, we can see that *obstinate* must mean *stubborn*.

DIRECTIONS Read each sentence and study the context. Write the meaning of the underlined word on the line below.

1. The solos by Ilona on the violin and Darin on the cello were <u>highlights</u> of the orchestra's performance.

   _____

2. The New York Symphony Orchestra gave such a <u>dazzling</u> performance that everyone sat in total silence to avoid missing a note.

   _____

DIRECTIONS Read each sentence. Then circle the meaning of the underlined word.

1. Ron's <u>vision</u> changed and now he needs glasses.

   thinking   eyesight   health

2. The <u>anxious</u> boy did not want to wait until his birthday to open his presents.

   angry   eager   sad

3. Mary is said to be <u>humble</u> because no one has ever heard her brag.

   well-known   modest   complaining

4. Samantha read with great <u>curiosity</u>, studying every word and situation carefully.

   surprise   danger   interest

5. The long <u>journey</u> to England was filled with miles of dangerous, winding roads.

   trip   highway   city

6. The new symphony was a <u>tremendous</u> success enjoyed by everyone.

   disputed   near   great

7. The <u>oration</u> lasted almost four hours, and I was surprised the man had any voice left.

   exam   movie   speech

8. In the cave, the boys noticed the <u>phosphorescent</u> rocks lighting up the darkness.

   sharp   glowing   damp

9. That type of roof is <u>unique</u> since no other house in the neighborhood has one like it.

   expensive   old   one-of-a-kind

10. The <u>exultant</u> team leaped up and then danced onto the floor.

    screaming   happy   angry

11. The man seemed <u>disoriented</u> since he didn't know his name or where he was.

    confused   sick   lonely

12. I was <u>mesmerized</u> by the beauty of the music and wished it would never end.

    bored   disgusted   hypnotized

13. This composer will surely be <u>acclaimed</u> all over the world when people hear his magnificent work.

    ignored   honored   moved

Read and Apply

DIRECTIONS Read about a famous composer. Use context clues to help with unfamiliar words.

(1) Franz Joseph Haydn began his life in a humble cottage in the small village of Rohrau, Austria. Born on April Fool's Day in 1732, Haydn fooled everyone by becoming one of the world's most outstanding musical composers.

(2) When Haydn was only six years old, his schoolmaster-cousin recognized his talent and launched him on a musical path. Two years later, he was admitted to the emperor's Court Chapel in Vienna, Austria where he quickly became one of the star singers. Haydn stayed with the school choir until his voice changed and he was dismissed.

(3) At seventeen, Haydn found himself alone and penniless in the streets of Vienna. The years after he left the choir were difficult. He had to support himself by playing the violin at social functions, by giving lessons, or arranging short pieces of music. Although life was not easy, Haydn continued to study and practice. Slowly, his reputation grew.

(4) Eventually, Haydn received an appointment to work at the court of Prince Esterhazy in eastern Austria. At the time, the prince's palace was one of the most elaborate in Europe. It contained not only hundreds of guest rooms, but also a theater, a huge park, a library and a four-hundred seat opera house. No wonder the prince was named Nicolaus the Magnificent!

(5) Haydn was pleased with his new job, but it kept him very busy. He conducted the palace orchestra, which meant practicing every day with the musicians and singers. He had to compose most of the music the orchestra performed, and he had to take care of the music books and instruments. No great conductor today would be expected to do all these jobs. Even though he was probably rushed at times, Haydn rarely lost his patience. He was like a father to the musicians, and they fondly called him "Papa Haydn."

(6) Haydn remained at the palace for about thirty years. Although he was sixty years old when he finally left, Haydn was anxious to try something new. When John Solomon came from London to fetch him, Haydn eagerly embarked on the rough voyage across the English Channel. Even though Haydn could not speak English, he was entertained royally by the English people.

(7) Haydn's first performance in London was a tremendous success. The audience was so stirred by his new symphony that they gave him a standing ovation. The audience applauded until even the slow movement, usually the most uninspiring, was repeated.

(8) Haydn wrote twelve more symphonies during his visit to London. He developed the symphony from a short, simple form of music to the long form for large orchestras as we know it today. For this accomplishment, Franz Joseph Haydn has been called the "Father of the Symphony."

DIRECTIONS Read each word. Use the paragraph number in parentheses to find each word in the story. Read the word in context. Then write the meaning of the word on the line.

1. humble (paragraph 1) _____

2. launched (paragraph 2) _____

3. penniless (paragraph 3) _____

4. elaborate (paragraph 4) _____

5. conductor (paragraph 5) _____

6. fondly (paragraph 5) _____

7. fetch (paragraph 6) _____

8. embarked (paragraph 6) _____

9. stirred (paragraph 7) _____

10. ovation (paragraph 7) _____

11. developed (paragraph 8) _____

12. form (paragraph 8) _____

13. accomplishment (paragraph 8) _____

REMEMBER Read all the words to get an unknown word's meaning.

It All Adds Up

Would you have much money if you placed one penny next to two pennies, then stacked four pennies, then eight pennies and continued to double the amount for row after row? In this lesson, you'll read about how quickly pennies add up as you learn to use many words to figure out the meaning of one word.

 ## 1 KEYS to Multiple-Meaning Words

Some words can mean several different things.

LEARN   Many words have more than one meaning. When you read a multiple-meaning word, you need to see how the word is used in the sentence to know which meaning is meant.

EXAMPLE   When *strike* is used to talk about baseball, it means the ball has been pitched so it could have been hit. A *strike* by workers, however, is when they refuse to work. You aren't supposed to *strike* another person, but fishermen love it when a fish *strikes* their line.

DIRECTIONS   Read the paragraph. Then read each word and its meanings. Circle the letter of the meaning used in the paragraph.

While serving in the military in Germany, I was stationed at a small base where I was involved in scientific and mathematical study. I analyzed samples of earth, while several friends wrote manuals about navigating the stars. All the work was used to assist aircraft pilots.

1. earth: **a.** a planet   **b.** dirt
2. base: **a.** safe area in baseball   **b.** military post
3. stars: **a.** suns in the sky   **b.** famous people
4. pilots: **a.** leaders   **b.** those who fly planes
5. serving: **a.** presenting food   **b.** doing a duty

2 Practice With Multiple-Meaning Words

DIRECTIONS Read each word and its meanings. Then read each sentence. Write the letter of the underlined word's meaning on the line.

grate **a.** frame of metal bars **b.** to grind into bits **c.** to annoy

mandarin **a.** small, sweet orange **b.** official language of China

warrant **a.** deserve **b.** a promise or guarantee **c.** an official paper giving permission

assembly **a.** a gathering **b.** fitting parts together

surface **a.** the outside of **b.** to come out of hiding **c.** outward appearance

_____ **1.** Perhaps nothing <u>grates</u> a person's nerves more than the sound of fingernails scraping down a chalkboard.

_____ **2.** The orchestra played for our all-school <u>assembly</u> today.

_____ **3.** Your good behavior <u>warrants</u> a special privilege.

_____ **4.** The <u>grate</u> under the refrigerator door needs to be cleaned.

_____ **5.** I could easily eat the whole jar of <u>mandarins</u>.

_____ **6.** The truth will <u>surface</u> eventually.

_____ **7.** I can't figure out the directions for the <u>assembly</u> of this new gadget.

_____ **8.** He is all smiles on the <u>surface</u>, but I know he is angry about something.

_____ **9.** Our new student speaks <u>Mandarin</u>, French, and English.

_____ **10.** The <u>surface</u> area is the sum of the areas of all the sides.

_____ **11.** This recipe calls for <u>grated</u> lemon and orange rinds.

3 Read and Apply

DIRECTIONS Read how it all adds up. Watch for multiple-meaning words.

Long ago, a young man was passing through an English forest on horseback when he heard a woman call out for help. He moved cautiously in the direction of the cries until he came upon a pair of bandits who were holding a woman at gunpoint. The young man leveled his musket and told the robbers to drop their weapons. The woman rushed forward to thank the stranger. She told him she was the king's daughter. She said her father would reward this unusual bravery.

The king was playing chess when the news of his daughter's rescue reached him, and he immediately summoned the youth.

"You have done me a great service," the monarch said. "What would you ask of me?"

The young man thought a moment before pointing to the chessboard. "Only a few cents, Sire," he said. "If you would merely place one penny on the first square of that board, two pennies on the next, four on the next, and so on, doubling the number each time, I would be well enough rewarded."

The king considered this a small enough price to pay for his daughter. In fact, he smiled to himself at how little the youth had requested.

"Done!" he cried, and he called at once for the Royal Treasurer to add the number of pennies.

The treasurer began to add. He added and added and added. Then he added some more. He scratched his head and looked at his figures. Then he checked his record by adding it a second time. When certain his total was correct, the treasurer handed the paper to the king, who looked at it first with surprise and then with sorrow. The amount he had promised to pay was greater than the value of his entire kingdom!

Multiple-Meaning Words **39**

Find each word in the story you just read and circle it. Then circle the letter of the word's meaning as it was used in the story.

1. call:　**a.** shout　**b.** communicate by phone
2. leveled:　**a.** pointed　**b.** torn down
3. playing:　**a.** pretending　**b.** participating in a game or sport
4. reached:　**a.** put a hand out to take hold　**b.** traveled to
5. forward:　**a.** a basketball player　**b.** ahead
6. service:　**a.** a soldier's profession　**b.** a useful act
7. thought:　**a.** an idea　**b.** to think
8. monarch:　**a.** a type of butterfly　**b.** a ruler
9. before:　**a.** in front of　**b.** previously
10. scratched:　**a.** rubbed　**b.** marred on the surface
11. youth:　**a.** being young　**b.** a young person
12. head:　**a.** a chief or ruler　**b.** a part of the body
13. place:　**a.** a location　**b.** put
14. holding:　**a.** not letting go　**b.** waiting
15. paper:　**a.** a news publication　**b.** a sheet for writing
16. reward:　**a.** payment　**b.** to give praise or money for a good deed
17. value:　**a.** worth　**b.** to treasure
18. surprise:　**a.** do without telling　**b.** amazement
19. rescue:　**a.** to save　**b.** the act of saving
20. figures:　**a.** shapes　**b.** numbers
21. record:　**a.** a flat plastic disk　**b.** a written report
22. correct:　**a.** right　**b.** to fix or repair

DIRECTIONS Write the meaning of the underlined word as used in each sentence.

1. May I have a <u>stick</u> of gum?

_____

2. I have my skates and hockey <u>stick.</u>

_____

3. Don't <u>stick</u> anyone with that job!

_____

4. Good friends <u>stick</u> together.

_____

5. Don't <u>stick</u> your nose into my business.

_____

REMEMBER Read the whole sentence to get a word's meaning.

Circles of Terror

The Oxford English Dictionary gives over 800 meanings for *run* and forms of the word like *ran* or *running*. In this lesson, you will learn about words with multiple meanings. You'll also read about how terrifying nature can be.

1 KEYS to Multiple-Meaning Words

A word's meaning often depends on the words around it.

LEARN Many words have more than one meaning. When you read a word that has several different meanings, you use the context, or words around the multiple-meaning word, to figure out its meaning.

DIRECTIONS Read the paragraph. Then read the two definitions for each word. Circle the letter of the meaning used in the paragraph.

Jerry almost cried. How could he perform the lead in the play wearing this ugly costume? The bear suit was so big and baggy it almost looked like a dress. It tied in the back with little bows. Jerry was in a state of depression as he wore the costume out to show his teacher.

"Don't worry, Jerry," said Mrs. Sims, trying not to laugh. "We'll put it right back in the box and ship it out. By the night of the play, you'll have a super costume."

1. bear: **a.** a furry animal **b.** to carry
2. ship: **a.** an ocean vessel **b.** to send
3. lead: **a.** the main part **b.** to show others the correct way
4. dress: **a.** put on clothes **b.** a piece of female clothing
5. box: **a.** to fight **b.** a container

2 Practice With Multiple-Meaning Words

DIRECTIONS Read each word and its meanings. Then read each sentence and write the number of the word's meaning on the line.

degree 1. a step in a series 2. a rank earned by a student 3. a measure of temperature

_____ **A.** Mrs. Kearns has a master's degree in education.

_____ **B.** I like scary movies to a degree.

_____ **C.** He's surely going to be recommended for a degree.

_____ **D.** It is currently ten degrees above normal.

external 1. on the outside 2. on the outside of the body 3. an influence outside of oneself 4. having to do with foreign countries

_____ **A.** His dad is involved in the external policies of our country.

_____ **B.** An external force must be causing his strange behavior.

_____ **C.** This lotion is for external use only.

_____ **D.** The crust is the external layer of the earth.

reciprocal 1. given in return 2. working together as with parts of a machine 3. one of a pair of numbers which, when multiplied together, yield a product of one

_____ **A.** We had a reciprocal agreement to help each other with homework.

_____ **B.** The chain and sprocket are reciprocal parts of a bicycle.

_____ **C.** This math assignment will help us understand reciprocals.

_____ **D.** The reciprocal of 1/3 is 3.

possess 1. to own something 2. to have as part of oneself 3. to have power or control over

_____ **A.** Mildred has shown that she possesses compassion.

_____ **B.** We were possessed by fear when we heard the groaning sound.

_____ **C.** I must admit I would love to possess all those things.

_____ **D.** Tyrone is possessed by the desire to win.

Look for words with multiple meanings as you read about circles of terror.

People who live in the tropics fear one thing above all else—hurricanes. Each year these circular storms cause millions of dollars in damage and often take a toll of human lives. It is impossible to tell where a hurricane will strike. All that is known is that hurricanes originate near the equator in an area known as the Torrid Zone.

One breed of storm has three different names. In the Atlantic area, hurricanes cause terror. The same type of storm, a typhoon, is devastating in the North Pacific, and cyclones are feared in the South Pacific.

When air masses moving in opposite directions come together, the result can be a circular movement that could become a hurricane. A full-grown hurricane measures hundreds of miles across. Its winds might exceed 200 miles an hour but need only reach 73 miles per hour to qualify as hurricane force. At the center of these winds is the storm's eye, an area of surprising calm where air pressure forms an extreme low. The eye is surrounded by a wall of clouds that whirl with a fierce destructive force. This energy causes ocean waves to rise several feet above normal in what is called a storm surge. When a surge reaches land, severe flooding, the single greatest cause of death from a hurricane, can result.

Scientists seed a hurricane's clouds in an effort to make it rain and thereby rob the storm of its force. Satellites photograph the storm from space and make it possible to predict with reasonable precision when and where the hurricane will strike.

When a warning goes out, people board up their windows and take their valuables inland. Ships in the harbor sail into the open sea to avoid being battered against shore. These monstrous storms cannot be leashed. The best advice is to stay as far as possible from the "circles of terror."

Read the different definitions of the words below. Then write the meaning that was used in the article you just read on the lines.

- The *area* is the amount or size of a surface measured in square units.

- An *area* is a region or a part of the earth's surface.

- A *board* is a long, flat, broad piece of wood used for building purposes.

- A *board* is a flat piece for a special purpose such as ironing, chess, etc.

- To *board* is to provide food and a place to sleep in exchange for payment.

- To *board* is to cover something up with long, flat pieces of wood.

- A *board* is a group of people who manage or control.

- A *surge* is a sudden, strong rush of energy.

- A *surge* is a large wave of water in a violent, rushing motion.

- A *force* is the power or energy that makes something happen.

- A *force* is a group of people working together for a common purpose.

- To *force* is to use strength or power to cause something to occur.

- *Warning* is the act of telling of a danger.

- A *warning* is something that tells of a danger or an event to come.

- An *eye* is the part of the body that allows one to see things.

- The *eye* is the central part of something.

- To *eye* something is to look at it carefully or critically.

- A *single* person is one who is not married.

- *Single* is one and no more of something.

- To *single* out is to select one from all the others.

- A *seed* is part of a flowering plant that will produce a new plant.

- To *seed* is to take an action in hopes of making something happen.

- The *seed* is the source or the beginning of something.

- To *seed* is to remove the seeds from a fruit or vegetable.

1. warning _____

2. single _____

3. area _____

4. board _____

5. surge _____

6. seed _____

7. force _____

8. eye _____

REMEMBER A word's meaning depends on how it's used in a sentence.

Mountains of Fire

Some mountains have "tempers" that flare up occasionally. In this lesson, you'll read about these temperamental mountains as you learn about words that have more than one meaning.

1 KEYS to Multiple-Meaning Words

A word may have many different meanings.

LEARN   Many words in the English language have more than one meaning. A word with multiple meanings is often used as a *noun* for one meaning and as a *verb* for another meaning. As a noun, the word names a person, place, or thing. When used as a verb, the word expresses action.

EXAMPLE   The *desert* was *deserted*.

Desert is a noun naming a hot, dry place. The verb *deserted* means *to leave or abandon*.

DIRECTIONS   Read each word and its two meanings. Write *noun* on the line after the noun meaning and *verb* after the verb meaning.

1. water: **(a)** a chemical substance necessary for life

   _____

   (b) to wet something with water

   _____

2. shade: **(a)** an area out of the sun

   _____

   (b) to add detail to a painting

   _____

Practice With Multiple-Meaning Words

DIRECTIONS To determine the intended meaning of a multiple-meaning word, use the context, or the other words around it. Use context to find the meaning of the underlined word in each sentence. Mark an *X* in the correct column to show how the word is used.

Noun   Verb

_____   _____   **1.** After washing the car, <u>rinse</u> it with water from the hose.

_____   _____   **2.** I used light brown to <u>shade</u> the picture I was painting.

_____   _____   **3.** In my house, each school picture is put in a <u>frame</u> and hung on the wall.

_____   _____   **4.** For science class, we are going to make a collection of <u>bugs</u>.

_____   _____   **5.** Farmer Brown keeps his pigs in a <u>pen</u> by the barn.

_____   _____   **6.** My math teacher told me this <u>type</u> of problem is difficult.

_____   _____   **7.** My baby sister is determined to <u>bug</u> my friends and me.

_____   _____   **8.** The meal was served with a loaf of hot bread and a <u>knife</u> which was quite sharp.

_____   _____   **9.** My brother has learned to <u>type</u> at a rate of sixty words per minute.

_____   _____   **10.** The football player <u>knifed</u> through the line and darted down the field.

_____   _____   **11.** My sister used a cream <u>rinse</u> on her hair last night.

_____   _____   **12.** On behalf of our class, we <u>presented</u> a plaque to the school.

_____   _____   **13.** What is all the <u>fuss</u> and commotion out here?

_____   _____   **14.** There's a handsomely-wrapped <u>present</u> on the table.

_____   _____   **15.** The babies <u>fussed</u> continually through the ceremony.

3 Read and Apply

DIRECTIONS Read about mountains of fire.

Most mountains are formed slowly by the action of continental movement. Others are formed with astonishing speed as molten rock reaches the earth's surface through a weak point in its crust. These mountains, called volcanoes, can be very dangerous to people, animals, and plants that are hundreds of miles away. A huge eruption 700,000 years ago in what is now California sent clouds of ash as far east as present-day Kansas.

Although there is less volcanic activity today than in the remote past, many dangers still exist. An eruption on the island of Java in 1982 left 30,000 people homeless. Another 20,000 people had to be evacuated from the area near Mt. Chichon, in Mexico, during that same year. In the U.S., the explosion of Mt. St. Helens in 1980 caused $1.6 billion in damages, and geologists say the worst may yet lie ahead for the Western United States. Perhaps the major reason volcanoes are so destructive is that the long, peaceful periods between eruptions lull people into the belief that volcanoes are not dangerous. Entire cities may be built within view, or even on the slopes, of a volcano.

There are about 600 active and 10,000 inactive volcanoes today. Most are located in three belts. One belt, called the *ring of fire,* circles the edge of the Pacific Ocean. A second belt reaches from the Mediterranean to the East Indies, while a third lies along the mid-ocean ridges. These areas are also associated with earthquakes.

The highest volcano in the world is Chimborazo, in Ecuador. The highest in the United States is Mt. Wrangell, in Alaska, where a number of other volcanoes can be found. In the Continental U.S., the highest is Mt. Baker in Washington. Mt. St. Helens, also in Washington, had this distinction until 1980, but it lost 1,500 feet of its height when it exploded and its entire top was vaporized.

Read each word and its meanings. Write *verb* on the line after the verb meaning and *noun* after the noun meaning. Then write the number of the correct definition as used in the article you just read.

_____ **A.** surface   **1.** to come to the top of _____

     2. the outer face _____

_____ **B.** speed   **1.** to travel at a fast rate _____

     2. quickness _____

_____ **C.** point   **1.** an exact location _____

     2. to indicate a position by extending a finger _____

_____ **D.** damages   **1.** money paid for destruction done _____

     2. hurts or breaks _____

_____ **E.** lie   **1.** an untruth _____

     2. to be or exist _____

_____ **F.** view   **1.** sight _____

     2. to look at _____

_____ **G.** lull   **1.** quiet time _____

     2. gently calm _____

_____ **H.** number   **1.** a quantity _____

     2. to count while assigning numbers _____

DIRECTIONS Read each sentence. Write *N* on the line before the sentence if the underlined word is used as a noun. Write *V* if the word is used as a verb.

_____ **1.** We couldn't understand the toddler's jabber.

_____ **2.** There were seven candidates on the slate for president of our class.

_____ **3.** Please phrase your question differently.

_____ **4.** The hunting lodge provided excellent accommodations.

_____ **5.** Mom will grind the coffee beans she purchased in Columbia, South America.

REMEMBER Some words can be used as nouns or as verbs.

Let the People Decide?

When half the people choose one thing and the other half chooses another, there can be no decision. In this lesson, you'll read about people trying to decide how to pronounce their state's name. You'll also learn about words with more than one meaning.

 ## 1 KEYS to Multiple-Meaning Words

Words often have more than one meaning.

LEARN Several meanings may be given for a word in the dictionary. Each numbered definition follows an abbreviation which tells the part of speech for that definition. *Adj.* is for *adjective,* or a word that describes a noun, *v.* is for verb or an action word, and *n.* is for noun or the name of a person, place, or thing.

EXAMPLE **foul** *adj* 1. dirty, smelly, rotten. 2. stormy. 3. unpleasant. *v.* 1. to make dirty. 2. to hit a ball out of bounds. *n.* 1. a ball hit out of bounds. 2. an act that is against the rules.

DIRECTIONS Use the dictionary entry above to answer the questions.

1. How many verb meanings are given? _____

2. How many noun meanings are given? _____

3. How many adjective meanings are given? _____

4. When *foul* is used to describe nasty weather, what part of speech is the word?

_____

5. What is the third adjective meaning?

_____

Practice With Multiple-Meaning Words

DIRECTIONS Read the dictionary entries. Then read each sentence. Write *noun*, *adjective*, or *verb* on the line below to tell the part of speech for the underlined word. Write the word's meaning on the line.

initial *adj.* first. *n.* the first letter of one's name. *v.* to mark with the first letter of one's name.

salvage *n.* 1. the act of saving a ship and its contents from danger. 2. goods saved from a wreck. *v.* 1. to save from damage. 2. to use what can be saved.

supplement *n.* 1. something added to make up for something missing. 2. a section added to give special articles or up-to-date information. *v.* to add to.

potential *adj.* possible. *n.* power or skill that may be developed.

function *n.* 1. special work or purpose. 2. a formal party or important ceremony. *v.* 1. to act or do its work. 2. to be used.

1. This machine will not <u>function</u> properly.

   a. part of speech _____

   b. meaning _____

2. I read an article about Arkansas in the newspaper <u>supplement</u>.

   a. part of speech _____

   b. meaning _____

3. Our <u>initial</u> test was more difficult than this one.

   a. part of speech _____

   b. meaning _____

4. My coach says I have real <u>potential</u> as a pitcher.

   a. part of speech _____

   b. meaning _____

5. We will <u>salvage</u> everything we can before the building is torn down.

   a. part of speech _____

   b. meaning _____

Read and Apply

 Look for words that have multiple meanings as you read about a state that couldn't agree on how to pronounce its name.

A century ago, people in the state of Arkansas argued heatedly about how the name of their state should be pronounced. About half the people felt the accent should fall on the first syllable and that the last syllable should sound like *saw*. The other half of the residents thought the accent should fall on the second syllable. The last part of the state's name would then sound like *Kansas*.

The dispute grew to such proportions that the people decided the question needed an official answer. They looked to the state legislature to decide the pronunciation. A committee of legislative members was appointed to study the matter. The committee wrote a letter to the great American poet, Henry Wadsworth Longfellow, who lived in Maine and had never been to Arkansas. They asked Longfellow which pronunciation he would recommend. In his reply, he told the committee that placing the accent on the first syllable seemed to produce a more musical and poetic sound. The legislature took Longfellow's advice and passed a law establishing the offical pronunciation of the state's name. Hereafter, Arkansas would be pronounced with the accent on the first syllable.

Outside Arkansas, however, some people still prefer the other pronunciation. The Arkansas River, which begins in Colorado, undergoes a name change when it flows into Kansas. There it is pronounced with the accent on the second syllable so its name seems to contain the word *Kansas*. When the river flows out of Kansas and into Oklahoma, its name changes again.

Read each word from the story about Arkansas. Decide which of the word's definitions is used in the story. Underline the correct meaning.

A. matter *n.* 1. any substance made of atoms. 2. an issue, question or controversy. *v.* to mean something important.

B. produce *v.* to make or manufacture. 2. to manage or supervise. *n.* vegetables and fruit delivered to market.

C. state *n.* 1. the central government, referred to in general. 2. one of the fifty United States. 3. the government of the entire nation. *v.* to declare.

D. reply *v.* to respond in speech or writing. *n.* a verbal response, spoken or written.

E. accent *n.* 1. stress given to a particular syllable in a word when spoken. 2. a special way of pronouncing words used by people in particular regions. 3. a stress in the rhythm of music. *v.* 1. to pronounce with stress. 2. to mark with a special mark to show where stress is used in speaking.

F. study *v.* 1. to try to learn. 2. to look at carefully. 3. to take a course in. *n.* 1. the act of trying to learn. 2. deep thought. 3. a room set aside for reading, etc.

G. official *n.* 1. a person who holds an office such as in government. 2. a person whose job it is to see that rules are followed. *adj.* 1. formal or specific. 2. having to do with an office. 3. coming from a person in charge.

H. placing *v.* 1. putting. 2. finishing in a certain order. 3. identifying. *n.* a position in order.

I. passed *v.* 1. went by. 2. handed out or distributed. 3. successfully completed. 4. voted for and approved.

J. question n. 1. something asked in order to learn. 2. a matter to be decided. *v.* 1. to ask for information. 2. to doubt. 3. a problem.

DIRECTIONS Read about the uses of the word *objective*. Then read each sentence. Decide the part of speech used. Write it on the line.

When the word *objective* is used as a noun, it means *a goal or purpose,* but when used as an adjective, it means *not having or showing a strong opinion for or against something.*

_____ **a.** I was really trying to be objective about it.

_____ **b.** Mark has to meet two objectives in this course.

REMEMBER A word has different meanings in different situations.

Who's Afraid of a Number?

Many of our combining forms, or word parts, have been borrowed from the ancient Greek and Latin languages. We use these combining forms to build more words. In this lesson, you will learn the meanings of several combining forms as you read about a strange fear some people have.

1 KEYS to Word Parts

Combining forms have special meanings.

LEARN Combining forms have special meanings. Knowing these meanings can help you understand the meanings of new words in which they are used.

EXAMPLE The word *thermometer* is made from two combining forms, *therm* and *meter*. *Therm* means *heat* and *meter* means *a device for measuring*. A thermometer is a device for measuring heat.

DIRECTIONS Study the list of combining forms, their meanings, and example words. Choose three of the example words and write sentences using them. A dictionary may help.

Combining Form	Meaning	Example Word
astro-	star	astronaut
hydro-	water	hydroplane
-logy	study of	biology
-phobia	fear of	claustrophobia
photo-	light	photocopy
pyro-	fire	pyrotechnics
tri-	three	tricycle

1. _____.

2. _____.

3. _____.

② Practice With Word Parts

DIRECTIONS Complete the following sentences by choosing the best word from the list under each sentence. Use the combining forms on page 53 to help you.

1. Astrology is the study of the _____ .
       sun   stars   moon

2. People who have hydrophobia _____ water.
       enjoy   need   fear

3. A photon is a measure of _____ .
       light   heat   sound

4. A person who suffers from _____ would probably not take a job as a fire fighter.
       photophobia   pyrophobia   claustrophia

5. Hydrology is the study of _____ .
       fire   water   light

6. A trilogy would contain _____ parts.
       three   one   four

7. A person with photophobia is afraid of _____ .
       water   stars   light

8. A hydrometer measures the weight of _____ .
       sand   liquid   chemicals

DIRECTIONS   Read about strange fears, including the fear of the number 13.

Everyone is afraid at times. It can be a good idea to fear things that may really harm us. Some people, however, have fears even when no threat exists. These people may be reasonable in every other way, but they cannot overcome their fears. Their fears are usually focused on objects or situations. People who have unreasonable fears generally try to avoid the objects or situations that frighten them. If they cannot avoid the thing that frightens them, they may exhibit strange behavior, such as trembling, excessive sweating, and rapid breathing.

The more common types of fears have been given names using the combining form *-phobia,* which means *fear of.* For example, *cynophobia* is an excessive fear of dogs, even those that are harmless. This word combines *cyno-,* meaning dog, and *-phobia. Hydrophobia* is an abnormal fear of water. *Pyrophobia* is a unreasonable fear of fire. *Claustrophoba* is a fear of closed or small spaces. Some other fears are *acrophobia, ailurophobia, gynephobia, heliophobia, neophobia, panphobia, pedophobia, photophobia,* and *xenophobia.*

One of the strangest fears is *triskaidekaphobia.* This the the fear of the number 13. A person with triskaidekaphobia will try to avoid any contact with this number. So many people fear the number 13 that it is common for buildings to omit a thirteenth floor. Hotels often skip from 12 to 14 when numbering rooms, because many people object to staying in a room 13. Of course, the common fear of Friday the thirteenth is related to triskaidekaphobia.

While few people admit having triskaidekaphobia, many people "play it safe" by staying away from the number 13 whenever possible! Do you?

The article you just read mentioned several types of fears, all ending with the combining form *-phobia*. Use the following list to combine the forms below with *-phobia*. Create words that will fit in each sentence.

acro-   (high)   neo-   (new)   photo- (light)
ailuro- (cat)   pan-   (everything)   pyro-   (fire)
gyne-   (woman)   pedo-   (children)   xeno-   (foreign)
helio-   (sun)

1. A person who is afraid to try new things, like new foods, might have

_____ .

2. A person who is afraid to go outdoors in the daytime might have either

_____ or

_____ .

3. A person who avoids children might have

_____ .

4. A person who is afraid to go to the top of a high building might have

_____ .

5. A person who avoids cats might have

_____ .

6. A person who does not want to sit around a campfire or in front of a fireplace might have

_____ .

7. A person who never wants to be near people from foreign countries might have

_____ .

8. A person who avoids women might have

_____ .

9. A person who is afraid of just about everything might have

_____ .

REMEMBER The special meanings of combining forms help us understand new words.

Artists Through the Ages

If a painter's medium, or material, is paint, what is a sculptor's medium? In this lesson, you'll learn a special way to show how things are related. You'll also read about some famous artists.

1 KEYS to Analogies

An analogy shows two similar relationships.

LEARN In an *analogy,* the relationship of the first two words is the same as that of the last two words. Analogies help us see relationships quickly.

> *Paper* is to *writer* as *clay* is to *sculptor.*

A piece of paper is a writer's tool, much as a lump of clay is a sculptor's. Other analogies can be written to show the relationships of the artists and their mediums:

> *Writer* is to *sculptor* as *paper* is to *clay.*
> *Sculptor* is to *clay* as *writer* is to *paper.*

When *writer* is the first of the two creators on the left side of the analogy, then the writer's tool is first on the right side.

DIRECTIONS Read each analogy to see the relationships. Then mark an *X* before each analogy that shows the *same* relationship in a different way.

1. Brush is to painter as chisel is to sculptor.

_____ **a.** Brush is to chisel as painter is to sculptor.

_____ **b.** Chisel is to painter as brush is to sculptor.

_____ **c.** Sculptor is to painter as chisel is to brush.

_____ **d.** Painter is to sculptor as brush is to chisel.

2 Practice With Analogies

DIRECTIONS An analogy can be written in a simpler form by substituting a colon for the words *is to* or *are to* and a double colon for the word *as.*

Mona Lisa is to da Vinci as *Pieta* is to Michelangelo.
Mona Lisa : da Vinci : : *Pieta* : Michelangelo

Read the paragraph. Then use the list of words to write an analogy in two different forms.

Norman Rockwell, a popular American painter and illustrator of the 1900s, painted realistic scenes of everyday people in everyday situations. His paintings frequently tell stories, often in humorous ways. Pablo Picasso, on the other hand, is best known for his abstract creations. Often considered the most famous painter of the 1900s, the Spanish-born Picasso's paintings, sculptures, and drawings are called abstracts since his objects and people are not real looking. **Answers may vary.**

abstract   Rockwell   realistic   Picasso

a. _____ : _____ : : _____ : _____

b. _____ : _____ : : _____ : _____

3 Read and Apply

DIRECTIONS Read about two artists of the Italian Renaissance.

This power of lords and kings was declining toward the end of the Middle Ages. In the late fourteenth century, a new awakening occurred in Europe and spread to all the world. The Renaissance, or rebirth, period lasted about three hundred years until the middle of the seventeenth century. Some of the greatest artists of all time were creating during the Renaissance period. Two of these genius artists were Leonardo da Vinci and Michelangelo Buonarroti.

Leonardo da Vinci was a man of many talents and interests. His wide interests and abilities could sometimes be a handicap, since he failed to complete many of the paintings he began. Still, da Vinci is known as perhaps the greatest genius that lived.

Born near Florence, Italy, in 1452, da Vinci moved all over Italy during his lifetime and died in France in 1519. Throughout his life, he kept a notebook of sketches of things that interested him. The subjects were many, since he was a scholar of architecture, music, physics, botany, geography, and geology, among others. A mechanical engineer, da Vinci expressed his art through painting and sculpting. He also designed various types of aircraft.

A curious experimenter by nature, da Vinci's experiments often harmed his painting career. When painting *The Last Supper* onto a wall in Milan, he sought to create a better quality paint. Because of his experiment, this famous painting is faded and cracked today.

Toward the end of his life Leonardo da Vinci predicted that if people did not stop warring among themselves, there would be no humans left on the earth. His wisdom shows in his art. His *Mona Lisa* remains a puzzle today as we wonder what da Vinci was saying in this most famous painting in the world.

Leonardo da Vinci was already an accomplished artist when Michelangelo Buonarroti was born near Florence in 1475. An argumentative person, Michelangelo spent much of his life traveling between Florence and Rome. Whereas da Vinci was known for his wisdom and many talents, Michelangelo was known for his power. He was an independent man whose personality shows in his art.

Michelangelo took on massive projects, some of which were too large for him to complete. He began a tomb for a Pope that was to have forty marble statues. After forty years, however, only a few were completed.

The ceiling of the *Sistine Chapel*, the statue of *David*, the *Pieta*, and the statue of *Moses* were all huge projects and examples of Michelangelo's talent for depicting the human body in paintings and sculpture. His figures show power, both in size and emotion.

Michelangelo died in 1564. Although his work in his last years still revealed great talent, it shows less violence and intense emotion. His earlier paintings and statues have always been more popular, perhaps because they instill greater emotion in the observer.

DIRECTIONS Write the correct word on the line to complete each analogy.

1. Middle Ages : _____ : : 13th Century : 16th Century
   a. 1800's **b.** Roman Times **c.** Renaissance **d.** 1900's

2. Michelangelo : power :: da Vinci : _____
   a. temper **b.** wisdom **c.** Florence **d.** weakness

3. da Vinci : _____ :: Michelangelo : 1564
   a. 1519 **b.** 1915 **c.** 1700 **d.** 1452

4. _____ : da Vinci :: *Moses* : Michelangelo
   a. *Sistine Chapel* **b.** *David* **c.** *The Last Supper* **d.** *Pieta*

5. *The Last Supper* : fading :: Pope's tomb : _____
   a. da Vinci **b.** completed **c.** unfinished **d.** Florence

6. Renaissance : _____ :: massive : large
   a. express **b.** accomplished **c.** architecture **d.** rebirth

DIRECTIONS Write an analogy to show each relationship.

1. The births of da Vinci and Michelangelo

   _____ : _____ :: _____ : _____

2. Famous works by Michelangelo and da Vinci

   _____ : _____ :: _____ : _____

REMEMBER An analogy shows how two relationships are alike.

Fun in the Summer Sun

Many of the things we do each day require the ability to follow directions. In this lesson, you will learn about following directions as you read about how to make a sun clock.

 ## KEYS to Following Directions

Read all directions first.

LEARN When you are following written directions, it is important to read all the directions carefully before you start. Then follow them carefully. Sometimes it may help to reread the directions.

DIRECTIONS Read and follow this set of directions:

1. Read all items before completing any of them.

2. Write the name of your school: _____

3. Write the name of your favorite holiday: _____

4. Add these numbers: 6, 98, 198, 5, 18. Write the total: _____

5. Write "I am following directions carefully," on the next line:

_____

6. Do only items 1 and 5.

What have you written down? Did you write only the words "I am following directions carefully." for item number 5?

2 Practice Following Directions

DIRECTIONS It is the last day of school and you can hardly wait for summer vacation to begin. Your teacher, however, has one more assignment for you to do. It is an assignment on following directions. Here is that assignment. Be sure to read and follow all the directions carefully. Mark your answers in the box.

2	4	6	8	73	87	91
	Q	R		S	T	

fun   walk   goat   vacation   frighten

1. If there are two numbers that equal 8 when added together and a word that rhymes with *sun,* draw a line under the rhyming word.

2. If there is a word that means the same as *scare,* a word that is the opposite of *run,* and a word that rhymes with *boat,* put a star above these three words.

3. If there are five words, four even numbers, two numbers that equal 14 when added together, and three numbers that equal 36 when multiplied together, circle the word that means the same as time off from school.

4. If there are four letters in sequence, four words that each contain a different vowel sound, and at least two odd numbers, put a box around the four letters in sequence and a circle around the smallest of the odd numbers.

5. If all the numbers added together total 261, put a circle around the number 2. If, however, the total of all the numbers added together equals 271, draw a box around the number 91.

6. If any of the single letters in the box are vowels, put a star over the letter T.

7. If any of the words listed in the box have more than two syllables, put a circle around the letter Q.

Read and Apply

Read about how to make a sun clock.

Sundials or sun clocks were used to tell the time of day long before clocks and watches were invented. You can make a device similar to the ancient sundials by following these directions.

First, you will need to assemble your materials. To make a sundial, you will need a paper plate, preferably one without any designs on it. You will also need two pencils and a watch or clock that can be used outdoors.

Next, locate a place outdoors that will be in the direct sun all day. Do not choose a place that will have shade at any time during the day. Also, choose a place that is not covered with cement or blacktop.

Find the middle of the paper plate and make a hole through it with one of the pencils. Now, keeping the pencil in the hole, push the pencil part way into the ground. The pencil will do two things. It will hold the plate in place, and it will make a shadow across the plate.

Using your clock or watch to determine the actual time, make the first marking on your plate at the beginning of an hour. For example, begin at 8:00, 9:00, or 10:00 instead of 8:15, 9:20, or 10:45. Using the second pencil, draw a straight line on the paper plate along the

shadow. Write down the time next to the line. Repeat these steps at the beginning of every hour.

At the end of the day, you will have made a sun clock. Notice that some of the lines are short and some are long. The shortest line is twelve o'clock noon.

The next time you use your sun clock, put your pencil back in the hole at the center of the plate. Place the line from the noon shadow so that it faces directly north. By looking at where the pencil's shadow is now hitting the plate, you can tell approximately what time it is.

1. The first thing you do when you make a sun clock is

   a. get the correct time.

   b. assemble your materials.

   c. find a sunny spot outdoors.

2. Assemble these materials:

   a. paper plate, scissors, clock or watch.

   b. paper plate, clock or watch, a pencil.

   c. paper plate, clock or watch, two pencils.

3. Find a spot for your sun clock that is

   a. in the direct sun all day.

   b. on blacktop or cement.

   c. under a tree.

4. The pencil in the middle of the plate will

   a. hold the plate in the ground.

   b. make a shadow across the plate.

   c. both a and b.

5. Mark the sun's shadow on the paper plate

   a. any time you think of it.

   b. every half hour.

   c. at the beginning of each hour.

6. When you want to use your sun clock to find out approximately what time it is, place it so the

   a. longest line faces north.

   b. shortest line faces north.

   c. shortest line faces the sun.

REMEMBER Take the time to follow directions carefully.

A Prehistoric Pair

Paragraphs are groups of sentences that work together to explain or support a topic or main idea. In this lesson, you will learn about the topic sentence of a paragraph as you read about two prehistoric animals.

 ## KEYS to Topic Sentences

A topic sentence expresses the main idea of a paragraph.

LEARN A topic sentence states the main idea of the paragraph. It tells the reader what the paragraph will be about, and helps the reader focus on the main idea.

EXAMPLE **(a)** The Siamese cat weighs five to eight pounds. **(b)** Cats vary greatly in weight. **(c)** Tigers can weigh as much as 500 pounds.

If these three sentences were together in one paragraph, sentence *b* would be the topic sentence. Sentence *b* would probably come first in the paragraph.

DIRECTIONS Read the following groups of sentences. In each group, one sentence is a topic sentence and the other two support the topic sentence. Write the letter of the topic sentence on the line.

_____ 1. **(a)** The Grand Canyon is a stunning example of erosion.
(b) In river beds we can see layers of stone that have been cut through.
(c) Water can cause soil and rock to erode away.

_____ 2. **(a)** Jupiter, Uranus, Neptune, and Saturn are giants.
(b) The outer planets of the solar system are not like the inner planets.
(c) Mercury, Venus, Earth, and Mars are much smaller.

Practice With Topic Sentences

DIRECTIONS Read each pair of sentences. One sentence is a topic sentence and the other sentence contains a supporting detail. Decide which sentence is the topic sentence and write its letter on the line.

_____ 1. **(a)** The dictionary provides useful information.

   (b) The meanings and pronunciations of words are listed.

_____ 2. **(a)** Van Cliburn, a pianist, won a major award at age 10.

   (b) Many children have been famous as musicians.

_____ 3. **(a)** Small cars are easier to park.

   (b) There are some advantages to owning a small car.

_____ 4. **(a)** A baby-sitter has many responsibilities.

   (b) A sitter should always know emergency numbers.

DIRECTIONS Read the following paragraphs, both of which need topic sentences. Write a topic sentence for each paragraph on the lines.

Topic Sentence: _____

_____

_____

I enjoy playing in the sand, building castles, and digging holes. I love watching the boats on the lake and the gulls on the rocks. The warm sun makes me feel healthy, and people on the beach always seem friendly.

Topic Sentence: _____

_____

_____

First, I rinse the car thoroughly. Then I use a soft sponge to soap the car well. I rinse again to remove the soap. Finally, I dry the car with a clean soft rag.

66 Main Idea/Details

Read and Apply

Read about two prehistoric animals, and how they differ from their modern relatives.

1. Fossil remains of two prehistoric animals, the early horse and the mammoth, show us that both were quite different in appearance from their modern relatives. The earliest horse, for example, was only between ten and twenty inches high. On the other hand, mammoths, which were early relatives of the modern elephant, were often much larger than today's elephants. They also had hairy bodies and much longer tusks.

2. The first prehistoric horse, the eohippus, looked more like a racing dog than a modern horse. It had an arched back and a short, blunt nose. It had four toes on its front feet and three on its hind feet. Each toe ended in a tiny hoof.

3. By about three million years ago, this early horse had evolved into a creature much like the horse of today. Its side toes eventually became short leg bones and its center toe became a hoof. Its legs became longer and its body became larger. Its short snout became a long nose. Its teeth became larger and flatter, more suitable for grinding grass.

4. Fossils show that horses once lived on every continent on the earth, except Australia. There were once huge herds in both North and South America, but by the time the first Europeans arrived in the New World, there were no horses on these two continents.

5. One of the best-known mammoths is the woolly mammoth, which lived in the arctic regions of the world. It was nine to ten feet tall at the shoulder. Its back sloped from shoulder to hindquarters. Its thick, shaggy coat helped keep it warm. Its huge, curved tusks probably helped it scrape snow and ice from the plants it fed on. One woolly mammoth tusk has been found that is more than sixteen feet long!

6. There were several other species of mammoths, and many were even larger than the woolly mammoth. The largest mammoth, the imperial mammoth, was about fourteen feet tall at the shoulder. It lived in the southern parts of North America.

7. Mammoths became extinct between 3000 and 4000 years ago. Many were hunted by early humans. Some may have starved to death. Others, trying to reach plants in marshy areas, sank into the soft mud and could not escape. Fossils of mammoths have also been found preserved in ice in arctic areas.

DIRECTIONS Use the article to complete the exercise. One sentence is given from each numbered paragraph in the article. If the sentence given is a topic sentence, write ''topic'' on the line. If the sentence is a detail write ''detail'' on the line.

1. The earliest horse, for example, was only between ten and twenty inches high.

_____

2. The first prehistoric horse, the eohippus, looked more like a racing dog than a modern horse.

_____

3. By about three million years ago, this early horse had evolved into a creature much like the horse of today.

_____

4. Fossils show that horses once lived on every continent on the earth, except Australia.

_____

6. It lived in the southern parts of North America.

_____

5. Its thick, shaggy coat helped to keep it warm.

_____

7. Mammoths became extinct between 3000 and 4000 years ago.

_____

REMEMBER A topic sentence can help you make sense of a paragraph.

The Continents

The earth's continents have changed a great deal over millions of years. In this lesson, you will learn about main ideas of articles as you read about the continents.

 1 KEYS to Main Ideas

Long selections have main ideas, too.

LEARN   Some main ideas are larger than others. A paragraph has a main idea, but so do longer passages, like articles, chapters, and books.

EXAMPLE   An article in your favorite magazine looks interesting. The first paragraph is about mammals, the second about fish, the third about birds, the fourth about reptiles, and the fifth about amphibians. What is the main idea of the entire article? It is about vertebrates, the large classification of animals that includes all the animals in each paragraph.

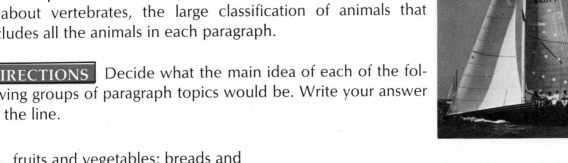

DIRECTIONS   Decide what the main idea of each of the following groups of paragraph topics would be. Write your answer on the line.

1. fruits and vegetables; breads and cereals; dairy products; fish, meat, poultry, and eggs

_____

2. roses, petunias, daisies, violets

_____

3. cats, dogs, hamsters, gerbils, parakeets

_____

4. canoes, sailboats, yachts, kayaks

_____

5. babies, boys, girls, men, women

_____

6. cows, pigs, horses, sheep, chickens

_____

2 Practice With Main Ideas

DIRECTIONS Read the list of topics and headings below. Make four groups of topics from the lists. Each group should have a heading, or subtitle, from the list which expresses the main idea of the group. Finally, choose a heading from the list which is the main idea, or title, of all the groups.

Isaac Asimov

Crazy Horse

Abigail Adams

United States First Ladies

Baseball Players

Ty Cobb

Nancy Reagan

Martha Washington

Native Americans

Eleanor Roosevelt

Dizzy Dean

Louisa May Alcott

Hank Aaron

A. A. Milne

Powhatan

Authors

Famous People

Tecumseh

Sitting Bull

Sandy Koufax

Judy Blume

Main idea, or title, of all groups:
_____

_____
Group 1 heading, or subtitle

_____

_____

_____

_____

_____
Group 2 heading, or subtitle

_____

_____

_____

_____

_____
Group 3 heading, or subtitle

_____

_____

_____

_____

_____
Group 4 heading, or subtitle

_____

_____

_____

_____

DIRECTIONS Read about the continents of the world, and how they have changed over millions of years.

A continent is a large mass of land that is one of the major divisions of the earth's land. Most people agree that there are seven continents: Africa, Australia, Europe, Asia, North America, South America, and Antarctica. Some geographers, however, think of Europe and Asia as one continent, called Eurasia. This is because no body of water separates the two continents. Other geographers think of Africa, Asia and Europe as one continent, since land connected Africa and Asia until the Suez Canal was built. This continent is called Eurafrasia. North and South America are also connected naturally by a narrow strip of land called the Isthmus of Panama. Australia and Antarctica are both completely surrounded by water.

Asia is the largest of the seven continents in land area, followed by Africa, North America, South America, Antarctica, Europe and Australia. Asia also has the highest population of the seven continents, as well as the greatest population density, or number of persons living per square mile. Antarctica has the lowest population. Because it is covered with ice most of the year, there is no permanent population in Antarctica.

For many years, it was thought that the continents had always been located where they are today. Now, however, most earth scientists believe that there was once one huge continent, called Pangaea. About 200 million years ago Pangaea began to break up, first into

two land masses called Gondwanaland and Laurasia, and then into smaller land masses that became continents. These smaller land masses drifted over a long period of time into their present locations and became the continents we know today. The rate of drift is very small, probably only one or two inches a year.

Using the theory of continental drift, earth scientists have predicted that millions of years from now the earth will look completely different than it does today. They believe that Africa and South America will move farther apart, and that Australia, which is now drifting north, may eventually bump into Asia. The California coast may separate from the mainland of the United States and drift toward Alaska.

Use the article to complete the exercise. Choose from the list a sub-title, or main idea, that best fits each paragraph and the whole passage. Write the sub-title on the line.

Description and Names of the Continents
How the Continents Have Changed
Formation and Movement of the Continents
Land Area and Populaton of the Continents
Major Land Masses of the Earth
Predictions for the Future of the Continents
The Continents, Their Sizes and Populations

1. First paragraph: _____

_____

_____

2. Second paragraph: _____

_____

_____

3. Third paragraph: _____

_____

_____

4. Fourth paragraph: _____

_____

_____

5. First two paragraphs: _____

_____

_____

6. Last two paragraphs: _____

_____

_____

7. Entire passage: _____

_____

_____

REMEMBER Paragraphs have main ideas, but so do longer passages such as articles, chapter, and books.

Unusual Facts About the United States

When you study a map, you may discover some interesting information. In this lesson, you'll learn about main ideas and details as you read some unusual facts about the United States.

 KEYS to Main Idea and Details

A main idea is supported by facts found in other sentences.

LEARN A main idea expressed in one sentence is usually supported by facts found in other sentences. Supporting details often follow the sentence that states the main idea.

EXAMPLE Main Idea: Death Valley is one of the hottest places on earth.
Detail: A temperature of 134 degrees Fahrenheit was once recorded in Death Valley.

In this pair of sentences, the first sentence expresses the main idea that Death Valley is one of the hottest places on earth. The second sentence supports that idea by showing an example of just how hot it can be in Death Valley.

DIRECTIONS Read each pair of sentences. Write D on the line in front of the sentence in each pair that is a supporting detail for the other sentence.

1. _____ On Yap Island large stones were once used for money.

   _____ Many types of objects have been used for money.

2. _____ Air travel has made much progress in a short period of time.

   _____ Only 66 years passed between the first airplane flight and the first manned landing on the moon.

2 Practice With Main Idea and Details

DIRECTIONS Read each group of sentences. Write M on the line in front of the sentence in each group that expresses the main idea of all the sentences in the group.

1. _____ Many people are driving smaller cars.

   _____ Higher oil prices have changed the way people live.

   _____ People are conserving fuel by using less for heating and cooling their homes.

   _____ Some people form car pools to drive to and from their work.

2. _____ A mixture of yellow and blue makes green.

   _____ A mixture of red and blue makes purple.

   _____ A mixture of red and yellow makes orange.

   _____ The three primary colors can be used to mix other colors.

3. _____ A well-balanced diet of nutritious foods is important for a strong, healthy body.

   _____ Fruits and vegetables have important vitamins and minerals.

   _____ Breads and cereals have carbohydrates that give us energy.

   _____ Meats and meat alternatives give the protein we need for growth and repair of body cells.

4. _____ Europe is really a peninsula of Asia.

   _____ North and South America are joined by a narrow strip of land called the Isthmus of Panama.

   _____ Australia and Antarctica are the only two continents that are naturally surrounded by water.

   _____ Before the Suez Canal was built, land connected Africa and Asia.

Read and Apply

Read to find out some interesting facts you can learn by looking at a map.

When Jim was assigned a report on the United States, he wasn't too surprised. What did surprise him was what the teacher said next. He wasn't allowed to go to the library. He wasn't allowed to use the encyclopedia. The only resource he was allowed to use was a United States map.

"This is going to be a very dull report," he thought. "Maps are boring." Then he found a map and began to study it. He knew he wouldn't find anything interesting about a map.

The first thing Jim noticed was that there is only one place where four states come together at a single point. The four states that meet are Utah, Colorado, New Mexico, and Arizona.

Then he paid attention to size. He noticed that the western states seem to be larger than the eastern states, and that Georgia is the largest state east of the Mississippi River.

Next Jim found some peculiar facts about direction. Even though Canada is north of the United States, there are places in Michigan where a person can travel south to reach Canada. In the southwestern corner of Arizona, it is possible to reach Mexico by traveling north. From Arkansas, a person can go in a southerly direction into all the bordering states—even Missouri, which is north of Arkansas.

The state borders were interesting, too. Every state but one has at least one straight line in its border. The only exception is Hawaii. Missouri and Tennessee border on the largest number of states (eight each). Maine, on the other hand, shares a border with only one state, while Alaska and Hawaii border on none.

Jim thought his report was pretty interesting, after all. It included many unusual facts that few people notice, even though they may have looked at a United States map many times.

Read each pair of sentences. Write D on the line in front of each supporting detail. Write M on the line in front of the main idea sentence.

1. _____ Jim wasn't allowed to use the encyclopedia.

   _____ Jim was surprised by his assignment.

2. _____ Jim thought nobody could find anything interesting on a map.

   _____ Jim thought his report would be dull.

3. _____ There is only one spot where four states come together.

   _____ One of those states is Utah.

4. _____ There was something interesting about the size of the states, too.

   _____ On the whole, western states seem to be larger than eastern states.

6. _____ In one place, Mexico is north of the United States.

   _____ Jim had to change some of his ideas about direction.

7. _____ It was interesting to look at the state borders.

   _____ Every state but one has a straight line in its border.

8. _____ A report on a map can be pretty interesting.

   _____ You can find interesting facts just by looking at a map.

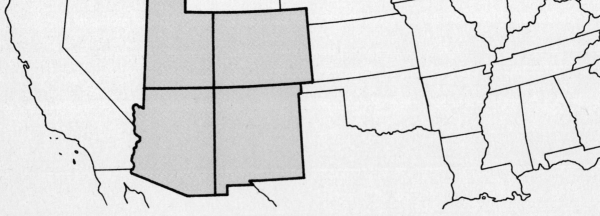

Supporting details give additional information about the main idea.

The Longhorn Trail

More than one hundred years ago, millions of fierce Longhorn cattle roamed the western plains. In this lesson, you will read about tough cowboys who moved these hardy cows over dangerous trails to northern market towns. You will learn about sequence, the order of events in a story.

1 KEYS to Sequence

The sequence of events tells what happened when.

LEARN Things that happen in a story are called events. A story has many events, and these events happen in a certain order. We call this order the sequence of events. Most stories have a "start to finish" sequence of events. The sequence of events can help you understand and remember a story.

Key words can help you follow the sequence of events. Words like *before, after, first, second, last, then, following, finally* and *later* help us understand sequence.

EXAMPLE Read this sentence carefully: A stampede of cattle often followed a loud clap of thunder. The word *followed* gives information about the sequence of events. It tells us that the stampede came after the thunder. The loud clap of thunder happened first.

DIRECTIONS Each sentence tells about two events. Use key words to figure out the sequence. Circle the letter that tells which part of the sentence happened first.

1. (A) The first cattle to reach North America came from Spain and (B) were later taken to Mexico.   A B

2. (A) Before railroads were built, (B) cowboys had to guide the cattle along dangerous trails to the northern market towns.
A B

DIRECTIONS The sentences below describe a day of yardwork, but they are out of sequence. First, read all the sentences carefully. Look for key words. Next, figure out the correct sequence. Then write the sentences in the correct order on the lines.

A. Finally I hosed down the whole area and headed to the park to play.

B. At last I was ready to drag the bags to the curb.

C. The first thing I did was pick up debris in the yard.

D. Before I did anything else on Saturday, I started my yardwork.

E. Then I raked the loose grass cuttings and bagged them.

F. Next I mowed the lawn.

G. Following a water break, which I deserved after mowing and raking, I cleaned the patio.

H. The second step was to sweep the cement blocks.

I. I started by scrubbing the lawn furniture.

1. _____

_____

_____

2. _____

_____

_____

3. _____

_____

_____

4. _____

_____

_____

5. _____

_____

6. _____

_____

_____

_____

7. _____

_____

_____

8. _____

_____

9. _____

_____

_____

DIRECTIONS Think about the sequence of events as you read a cowboy's story.

By the time round-up rolled around in the spring of 1880, I was already an old hand at driving herds of powerful Texas Longhorns from Texas to the market town of Abilene, Kansas. I had ridden the thousand mile long Chisholm Trail between Texas and Kansas more times than I could remember. Still I was always willing to risk taking another herd of Longhorns back to Kansas. I guess that's how I got the nickname "Kansas Mike."

That particular spring the Longhorns seemed especially independent. After the wild cattle were branded, counted and gathered together, we began the dangerous, three month journey north. The first two days we drove the Longhorns long and hard. We didn't want any of the leaders to recall what it was like to roam free. If they remembered and managed to turn the rest of the herd back towards their home range, we would never make it to market.

At the end of the first week, our herd was moving along as if it were on the open plain. We were using a secret I had learned from an old cowman: never let your herd know they are under control, and never let a Longhorn take a step unless it is in the direction of Kansas.

Later, when we reached Indian Territory, our trail boss was glad to pay the fee the Indians charged us to pass peacefully through their land. We had made it that far without a stampede, and were not going to dare the Indians to start one deliberately.

Yet anything could cause a stampede—hunger, thirst, lightning, a strange smell, or an unexpected noise. We worried that, no matter how well-behaved our herd seemed, they could all take off in a flash.

One unusually dark night, after the cattle were watered and bedded down, our worst fears became real. As our cook, Flapjack, walked behind the chuck-wagon, his foot slipped into a prairie dog hole. Involuntarily, he let out a cry of pain.

Instantly, thousands of sleeping Longhorns rose to their feet. As the thundering cattle headed toward us, I fought the urge to panic. Even with all my years of experience, there was nothing quite so frightening as the sight of so many racing Longhorns. Fortunately, our horses were always nearby, so I caught my breath and went galloping after them.

We spent the whole night yelling and slapping the cattle with our ropes. The herd ran for several miles before it eventually slowed down. Gradually, we turned the leaders and got the herd to run in a big circle. In the darkness, we couldn't tell how many of the Longhorns had escaped.

When daybreak came, we could see most of the cattle. They were grazing as if they had just awakened from a good night's sleep. As for me, I had lost my favorite hat, but felt lucky to have survived the great running herd of Longhorns.

When we finally reached Abilene, our herd was smaller, but it still brought a good price. As I watched the Longhorns enter the boxcars, I could only think about the next cattle drive north.

I didn't know then that several years later, Kansas would become my home. At the end of my last Longhorn drive, I settled in Abilene. Soon afterward the Chisholm Trail, and even the mighty Longhorns, were replaced by the railroads and other breeds of cattle. Only a few of my Abilene neighbors ever knew the real reason I was called "Kansas Mike."

DIRECTIONS   Number the sentences from 1 to 10 to show the correct sequence of events in the story.

_____ **a.** The cowpokes watched the Longhorns enter the trains.

_____ **b.** The trail boss paid the Indians to let the herd pass.

_____ **c.** In 1880, Kansas Mike was eager for the trail drive to start.

_____ **d.** Throughout the night, the cowboys tried to herd the Longhorns.

_____ **e.** Even after he left the cowboy life, Kansas Mike's nickname still fit.

_____ **f.** The herd seemed well-behaved after a week.

_____ **g.** Flapjack turned his foot in a burrow.

_____ **h.** At first, the cowboys drove the cattle as fast as they could.

_____ **i.** The Longhorns raced through the blackness.

_____ **j.** The cattle ate as if nothing had happened.

REMEMBER   Sequence is the order of events.

The Charles S. Wilson Fruit Jar Zoo

Charles thought about insects all the time. That was one of the reasons why Charles had problems in school. When the teacher was thinking of math and spelling, Charles was thinking of insects. In this lesson, you will read about how Charles started an insect zoo as you learn about the sequence of events in a story.

1 KEYS to Sequence

The order in which things happen in a story is called the sequence of events.

LEARN Things that happen in a story are called events. These events happen in order. This order is called the sequence of events. Understanding the sequence of events helps us understand the story.

Words like *before, after, first, second, finally, next, last, then,* and *later* give clues about sequence.

EXAMPLE Charles caught several insects after he fixed some bait.

The word *after* tells us Charles fixed bait first, and then caught insects.

DIRECTIONS Read each sentence. Then underline words that are clues to the sequence of events.

1. Charles started to collect insects after school ended for the summer.

2. Before he could go hunting for insects, Charles had to help his dad.

3. Charles' first insect hunting trip was not as successful as his second one.

4. The last insect Charles caught in the evening was a moth.

DIRECTIONS Read the beginning of the story about Charles and his insects.

At last school was out for the summer. Charles was finally free to do some serious insect hunting. All he needed were about a hundred more specimens, and he could open his insect museum in the garage. Every kid in town would come to see it. A lot of adults would come, too.

On the first Saturday afternoon of summer vacation, after he had helped his dad mow the lawn and trim hedges, Charles took a net and combed the high grass along the road. He came up with nothing he wanted to keep, but he was sure he had heard some crickets. "I think I need some bait," he thought.

Back in the kitchen, Charles put a banana, a couple of canned peaches, and some sugar into the blender. Then he added gobs of peanut butter. The machine whirled the ingredients into what looked like swamp mud. This went into an empty jar.

"What is that disgusting-looking stuff?" asked Marge, Charles' big sister.

"This is going to help me capture some great specimens tonight," answered Charles. "Want to come with me to see how my bait works?"

"No, thanks. I'm babysitting anyway, remember? Robbie's folks are going away for a couple of days. They're bringing him over here."

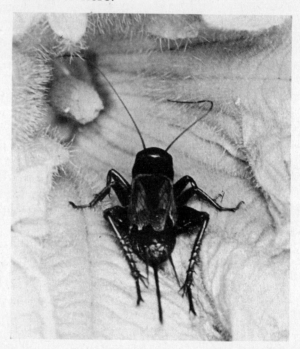

DIRECTIONS Number the sentences from 1 to 5 to show the correct sequence.

_____ Marge said she couldn't go with Charles because she had to babysit.

_____ Charles helped his dad mow the lawn and trim hedges.

_____ Charles returned home and made some bait in the blender.

_____ Charles went insect hunting after he helped his dad.

_____ Charles invited his sister to go with him on his second trip.

3 Read and Apply

DIRECTIONS   Finish reading the story about Charles and his insect zoo.

Just before dark, Charles walked to the tree he'd chosen for his experiment. He opened his jar and smeared the contents onto the tree trunk. Soon he saw a carpenter ant crawling toward his bait. He picked it up, examined it, and put it into a screened cage. Before he quit for the night, Charles had caught three more creatures, including a beautiful moth.

When Charles got home, Marge and Robbie were watching television. They didn't even notice Charles when he came in. He took his cage right to his room. As soon as he flicked on the light, he saw the mess. He couldn't believe it! The cards he'd mounted his insects on were scattered about the room. The insects he'd spent years collecting were all destroyed!

Robbie confessed. He told Charles he was sorry for wrecking the collection. Robbie said he'd thought the cards were like the pages in his see, feel, and smell book. He'd looked at, felt, and smelled the "bugs" on the cards. He didn't know he was "smushing" them.

Charles cleaned up the mess in his room, went to bed, and bawled. "This is the end," he thought. "There's no way I can capture and prepare enough insects for a display this summer." Then Charles decided to get up and look again at the beautiful insects he'd captured that night. After a while he began to feel better. It was impossible to look at the velvet wings of the moth and the shiny, strong bodies of the other insects and still feel upset. When Charles realized this, he got his brilliant idea. Of course! Why hadn't he thought of it before.

On July third, The Charles S. Wilson Fruit Jar Zoo opened. Mom and Dad welcomed the visitors. Robbie helped Marge serve punch and cookies. Inside the garage, the low shelves Charles had made by setting planks over cinder blocks held the collection. It was all contained in fruit jars and screened cages. Every specimen was alive. Underneath each jar and cage, the name of the inhabitant was printed on a card.

Sequence **83**

Most of the kids who came to the zoo liked the ladybugs and the praying mantis. The butterflies and crickets were popular, too. Of course, the punch and cookies were a big hit.

Charles grinned nonstop at his zoo's success. He decided he was going to release all his insects as soon as the show closed next week. After all, most of his family and friends would have seen them by then. And the insects deserved to be set free.

"This fruit jar zoo isn't what I first planned," he thought. "It's a thousand times better!"

DIRECTIONS Number each group of sentences 1, 2, and 3 to show the sequence in which the events occurred in the story.

A. _____ Charles went home and took his cage to his room.

_____ Charles saw a carpenter ant crawling toward his bait.

_____ Before he quit for the night, Charles had caught three more insects.

B. _____ Robbie confessed he had made the mess.

_____ Charles cleaned up the mess, went to bed, and bawled.

_____ Charles saw the mess in his room.

C. _____ Charles got up and looked at the beautiful insects.

_____ Charles got a brilliant idea.

_____ Charles began to feel better.

D. _____ Charles decided he would set the insects free after the show closed.

_____ Charles built shelves and made labels for his insects.

_____ The Charles S. Wilson Fruit Jar Zoo opened on July third.

REMEMBER Understanding the sequence of events helps to understand a story.

Why Babies Are Cute

People always seem to think babies are cute, don't they? This is not only true of human babies, but of many animal babies, too. In this lesson, you'll read about why babies have to be cute, and what they have in common that makes them seem lovable to us. You will learn about making inferences.

1 KEYS to Making Inferences

When you make inferences, you combine ideas.

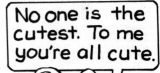

No one is the cutest. To me you're all cute.

LEARN   The answers to some questions are directly stated in what you read. These questions are called literal questions. Other questions have answers that are not so easy to find. You may need to combine two or more ideas that were in the passage. You may even need to think of some ideas of your own. When you do this, you are making inferences.

Study the cartoon and read the questions.

1. How many mice are in the cartoon?
2. What is the relationship between the big mouse and the little mice?

Question 1 is a literal question. All you have to do is to look at the cartoon and count the mice. To answer question 2, you must make an inference. You use ideas of your own, based on your experience with animals, to decide that the big mouse is the mother of the little mice.

DIRECTIONS   Answer the inference question about the cartoon in the example. Be sure to read the caption.

1. What do you think the little mice have been arguing about?

_____

_____

Practice Making Inferences

DIRECTIONS Read these paragraphs about the "cuteness" of pandas.

Why are stuffed panda toys so popular with "kids" of all ages? Why do most people think the panda is cute and cuddly, even when it's an adult? Some scientists believe this is because adult pandas have the same physical characteristics that most baby mammals have. These characteristics include a large, round head, big eyes, and a soft, round body.

The quality of keeping baby-like characteristics into adulthood has a fancy name—neoteny. Humans respond to this quality by wanting to treat the panda as they would a baby. They want to cuddle it and hug it. It's just as well that they settle for a stuffed panda, however, because it's not very smart to cuddle and hug any wild animal.

DIRECTIONS Answer each question. Then decide whether the question is literal or if you need to make inferences. If it is literal print an *L* on the line before the question. If it is an inference question, put an *I* on the line.

_____ 1. What baby-like characteristics does an adult panda have?

_____

_____

_____ 2. Which of the following animals is an example of neoteny? Circle the best answer.

    a. gorilla   c. bunny
    b. elephant

_____ 3. Why would it not be a good idea to cuddle a real panda?

_____

_____

_____ 4. The quality of keeping baby-like characteristics into adulthood is called

_____.

DIRECTIONS Read about the "cuteness" of baby animals, and how scientists think this quality may help them to survive their babyhood.

What is it about babies that makes them different from the adults of their species? Why do we so often think of them as being cuddly?

Animal scientists believe that the fact that babies are different from their parents is important to their survival. Their helpless cries, their appealing looks, and their cuddliness all help them to get the extra care they need to stay alive. This is particularly true of mammals and birds, who need more time to grow up than fish and reptiles do. If their parents did not take care of them, most bird and mammal babies would die. As they grow up, mammals and birds learn many survival skills from their parents. Fish and reptiles, for the most part, are born with the knowledge and physical abilities they need to survive.

It may also be possible that "cuteness" protects baby animals from being hurt by other members of their group. Most mammal babies are playful, curi-ous, and mischievous. They tumble into each other, and into the adults. They wrestle with and nip each other, as well as the adults. The adults generally put up with these annoyances from babies, but an older member of the group would probably get a good slap or bite, accompanied by a snarl, for such mischief.

What are some of the physical characteristics that distinguish animal babies from adults? Most mammal babies have heads that are larger and rounder, in proportion to their bodies, than they will have as adults. Their foreheads and their eyes are bigger, too, and their noses are smaller. Many have large, clumsy feet. Mammals that have fur as adults have softer, fuzzier fur as babies. Many primates, including humans, do not have as much body hair as they will have as adults. Some baby birds are born without any feathers at all. Others have soft down instead of feathers.

Some baby animals even have specially marked coats of fur, or are of a completely different color than their parents. A baby swan, for instance, has drab brown feathers rather than the beautiful white feathers it will have as an adult. Some baby chickens and baby ducks are bright yellow, but their adult feathers will be white or dark. A baby colobus monkey is completely white, whereas its parents are black and white.

When a baby animal begins to look more like a grown-up, it has already learned many adult behaviors and is treated more like an adult. If it continues to act like a baby, it will probably soon find itself in trouble!

DIRECTIONS   Answer each question. Some questions will have answers that are directly stated in the article. Others will have answers that will require you to make inferences. Circle *all* correct answers.

1. Which of the following animals would be likely to get special treatment from its parents because of its cuteness or helplessness?
   a. baby robin
   b. human baby
   c. baby tuna
   d. puppy

2. Which of the following characteristics do most baby animals have?
   a. large nose
   b. big ears
   c. long legs
   d. large forehead

3. A pair of kittens are playing together and one decides to bite its mother. What is the mother cat likely to do?
   a. Ignore the bite.
   b. Move away.
   c. Bite the kitten back.

4. A little swan is brown in color, rather than white. This shows that the swan:
   a. is an ugly duckling.
   b. is dirty.
   c. is a baby.

REMEMBER   An inference question takes more thought to answer than a literal question.

Booker's Dream

Booker T. Washington was born a slave and became a great American educator. In this lesson, you will learn about finding answers to questions as you read about Booker T. Washington.

KEYS to Making Inferences

Inferences help you answer hard questions.

LEARN The easiest questions to answer are questions whose answers are directly stated in the passages you read. Questions that require you to read, combine ideas, and make inferences can be more difficult. You need to think and search for answers.

DIRECTIONS Read the paragraph. Then read the questions. The answer to the first question is directly stated in the paragraph. The second question requires you to think and search. Write your answers on the lines.

The American Civil War began in 1861 and ended in 1865. On January 1, 1863, President Abraham Lincoln issued the Emancipation Proclamation, declaring that all slaves must be set free. This freedom did not come, however, until the war ended.

1. On what date did Lincoln issue the Emancipation Proclamation?

   _____

2. In what year did slaves actually become free?

   _____

DIRECTIONS Read about the slavery issue during the American Civil War.

One important cause of the American Civil War was that the nation was divided on the issue of slavery. The northern states wanted to abolish, or end, the slavery that the southern states had practiced for many years.

In the North, slavery had never been a necessary means of getting work done. Farms were small, and most of the farm work was done by members of the family. Northern cities had industries that hired laborers. In the South, however, the major activity was growing cotton. Cotton was grown on large plantations, and plantation owners depended on slaves to do the farm work.

DIRECTIONS The answers to the following questions are directly stated in the paragraphs. Write the answers on the lines.

1. What issue was one important cause of the American Civil War?

_____

2. On whom did plantation owners depend to do their farm work?

_____

DIRECTIONS Each of the following questions requires a "think and search" answer. Write your answers on the lines.

1. Why were the northern states anxious to abolish slavery?

_____

_____

_____

2. What were southern plantation owners afraid would happen if slavery was abolished?

_____

_____

_____

_____

DIRECTIONS Read about Booker T. Washington and how this former slave became one of America's greatest educators.

Blue morning glories climbed a trellis beside the porch of the cookhouse near a great southern mansion. Mockingbirds called from the giant trees. A young black boy of nine looked at his mother in amazement when she told him that they were now free from slavery. For many years the boy remembered how his mother looked that day in 1865 as she sat on a wooden bench shelling peas.

Jane Ferguson, the boy's mother, took her children to Malden, West Virginia, and soon the young boy was working in a salt furnace and a coal mine. When a night school for black children opened, the boy enrolled eagerly. Later, he arranged for day classes.

Strangely, the boy had gone for years without a real name. So when the teacher asked, he quickly made up a name for himself: Booker Washington. This had such a grand sound that his mother added a middle name, Taliaferro, from the name of a prominent Virginia family.

At the age of seventeen, Booker walked 300 miles to Hampton Institute, a school for blacks. The school officials were pleased with his attitude and they admitted him right away.

Booker worked as a janitor at Hampton until he graduated three years later. After he had taught school for a while at Malden, he became a professor at Hampton. His methods of teaching were gaining the attention of educators all across the United States.

The best was yet to come. Down in Tuskegee, Alabama, a banker received a charter to open a teacher's college and asked Hampton Institute for the best professor it could provide. Booker T. Washington was selected. At last, he had an opportunity to fulfill his dream of working with people of his own race in the deep South.

Arriving at Tuskegee, Booker's heart ached for his people. Forty eager students were crammed into a tiny shanty. Booker Washington went to work as never before. He took that tumbledown shanty and with much effort turned it into Tuskegee Institute, a fine college. He also wrote several books, including *Up From Slavery,* the story of his life.

As a boy, Booker had dreamed of getting an education. He not only fulfilled that dream, but he became one of the finest educators America has ever known. He died in 1915, a great and honored man, and was elected to the Hall of Fame in 1945.

DIRECTIONS Read each question. Write *directly stated* or *think and search* on the first line to tell what kind of answer is required. Then write the answer on the second line.

1. What was Jane Ferguson's work on the plantation?

_____

_____

_____

2. How did Booker T. Washington get his name?

_____

_____

_____

3. What are three ways in which Booker showed that he was not afraid of hard work?

_____

_____

_____

_____

_____

_____

_____

REMEMBER Some questions require you to combine ideas and make inferences.

The Sport of Fencing

The pirates and soldiers of bygone days fought death-defying duels with their swords. Today, however, fencing is considered a competitive sport. In this lesson, you will find out more about modern fencing. You will also learn about finding answers to literal and inference questions.

 ## KEYS to Making Inferences

Literal questions have directly-stated answers; inference questions require you to combine ideas.

LEARN Some questions are literal; their answers are directly stated. Other questions are inference questions. These require you to combine two or more ideas you have read, or to come up with ideas of your own.

DIRECTIONS Study the picture and read the caption. Then answer the questions.

Sword fighting used to be a survival skill. Today we only see this kind of fencing in movies.

1. What kind of skill was sword fighting in days of old?

   _____

2. What sounds would you expect to hear if you could get inside the picture?

   _____

2 Practice Making Inferences

DIRECTIONS Read these paragraphs about fencing and answer the questions.

"Duels to the death" with swords were very common in the 16th and 17th centuries. Even as late as the end of the 19th century, learning to fence was an important part of a gentleman's education, for he might have to use this skill to defend his honor.

Eventually, laws were passed that put an end to fencing duels, and firearms replaced swords on the battlefield.

Fencing is now considered a competitive sport. It was one of the first sports to be included in the modern Olympic Games. It is open to both men and women, but men and women do not compete against each other.

1. Would you be likely to see two people "dueling to the death" with swords today?

_____ Why or why not? _____

_____

2. Would you be likely to see a man fencing with a woman in the Olympic Games?

_____ Why or why not? _____

_____

3. Do you think two women would have settled a quarrel with a sword duel in the 17th century?

_____ Why or why not? _____

_____

4. Circle the weapons that were probably used in wars in the 16th and 17th centuries.

machine guns

axes

swords

knives

hand grenades

clubs

Read and Apply

DIRECTIONS Read about the modern sport of fencing.

The sport of fencing existed in Europe more than 600 years ago. Fencing guilds, or clubs, were especially popular in Germany. Swords used in sport fencing had blunt ends. While the object of dueling was to harm the opponent without being harmed, the object of sport fencing was only to touch the opponent with one's sword without being touched.

There are three types of swords used today in the sport of fencing. The first, called the foil, is the basic teaching weapon. It is a thin, flexible sword, with dull edges and a blunt point. In foil fencing, scores are made only when a fencer touches the opponent's torso, or body trunk, with his sword. Touches to other parts of the body do not count as scores.

Foil fencers wear padded metal jackets and protective face gear, as well as gauntlets, or long gloves, to protect their hands and arms. In foil fencing tournaments, the foil has an electronic tip connected to a scoring machine. When the tip touches the opponent's metal jacket, the machine tallies a score.

A more experienced fencer might use an épée (A-pay) for competition. An épée has a heavier and stiffer blade than a foil and is triangular in shape. Epée fencers can score points by touching the sword point anywhere on the opponent's body.

The third type of fencing weapon is called a saber, or sabre. Sabers have flexible triangular blades that are heavier than the foil or the épée. Saber fencers score points by touching either the point or the edge of the blade to any part of the opponent's body above his hips.

Fencing positions and movements have special names. At the start of a match, the two opponents face each other with their knees bent, just out of range of each other's weapons. This is called the en garde (on guard) position. The lunge is the basic method of attack. To lunge, a fencer pushes off with the back leg while stepping forward with the front leg. The sword is stretched out, or thrust, toward the opponent. The opponent tries to prevent a score by pushing the attacker's blade aside. This is called a parry.

The strategies of fencing take years to perfect. Well-coordinated hand and footwork, good timing, and fast thinking are all essentials to the fencer who wants to outwit his or her opponent.

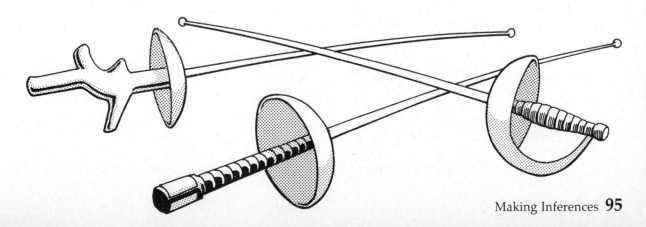

1. By touching the sword_____ anywhere on the opponent's body, épée fencers score points.

2. A fencer who scores a point by touching an opponent's leg with the edge of the sword would be using the

   _____ .

3. The sword most often used by beginning fencers is the

   _____ .

4. During which basic movement are the opponent's swords certain to be touching?

   _____ .

5. Fencer A lunges and attacks with a strong thrust. Fencer B parries. Fencer A's foil touches Fencer B's arm. Circle the letter of the answer that tells who will score.

   a. Fencer A
   b. Fencer B
   c. Neither Fencer A or B
   d. Both Fencer A and B

6. Why do you suppose fencing is sometimes called "physical chess"?

   _____

   _____

REMEMBER   Inference questions require you to think, reread, combine ideas, and use ideas of your own.

96 Making Inferences

Killer Whales

Our lives are filled with information. We get information from books, television, radio, newspapers, magazines, billboards, and other people. It is important to decide whether the information we receive is factual or if it is someone's opinion. Then we can make proper use of the information. In this lesson, you will read about killer whales as you learn about the difference between fact and opinion.

 ## KEYS to Fact and Opinion

A fact can be proved, while an opinion is a statement of belief that cannot be proved.

LEARN   A fact is a statement about a person, place, or thing. It can be proved true or false. An opinion cannot be proved. People have different opinions about the same subject.

DIRECTIONS   Read the sentences about horses. If the sentence is a fact, write *F* on the line. If the sentence is an opinion, write *O*.

_____ **1.** A horse is man's most faithful friend.

_____ **2.** Some horses perform in circuses and rodeos.

_____ **3.** The first horse was about the same size as a fox.

_____ **4.** There are different breeds of horses.

_____ **5.** No one could dislike a horse.

Practice With Fact and Opinion

DIRECTIONS Read these sentences about killer whales. If the sentence states a fact write *F* on the line. If the statement expresses an opinion write *O* on the line. Remember that words like *believe, feel, think, seem, might,* and *probably* are clues that the statement may be an opinion.

_____ 1. A newborn killer whale is about seven feet long and weighs approximately 400 pounds.

_____ 2. Some scientists think a whale can hear another whale's cry as far as ten miles away.

_____ 3. Probably the scariest thing about a killer whale is its name.

_____ 4. Killer whales feed on animals such as seals, fish, birds, dolphins, and even other whales.

_____ 5. People shouldn't be afraid of killer whales.

_____ 6. Killer whales can be taught to perform tricks.

_____ 7. Training a killer whale to do tricks is probably a lot of fun.

_____ 8. An infant whale grows two inches and gains one hundred pounds each day.

_____ 9. Killer whales can kill animals larger than themselves.

_____ 10. It is wrong to kill whales.

_____ 11. The sharp back fin of the killer whale often shows above the water when it is swimming.

_____ 12. Some fishermen believe killer whales are not worth hunting because they do not bring enough money when they are sold.

_____ 13. When a whale spots something to eat on top of ice, it charges the prey from underneath the ice.

Read and Apply

Read the story about killer whales. Be prepared to determine if the underlined sentences are facts or opinions.

Killer whales are aptly named because they are the top predators of the ocean. (1) They can count seals, dolphins, other whales and even ferocious sharks among their prey. For many years, scientists did not want to get too near killer whales. (2) No one would blame them for not wanting to be the hungry killer whale's next victim. (3) Yet, even though there are many gruesome tales about these animals, there are no proven records of killer whales attacking humans. In fact, scientists have found that killer whales hunt and kill mostly to keep themselves fed.

(4) Killer whales can be recognized by the black and white patches on their bodies. A killer whale can measure from 20 to 30 feet long and weigh from 3 to 7 tons. (5) It would seem that an animal this size would not be very speedy. However, as the killer whale swims along with its back fin poking out of the water as much as six feet, it looks like a sail boat racing along at speeds up to 35 miles per hour. (6) If you dare peek inside a killer whale's mouth, you would find rows of sharp, cone-shaped teeth that fit together like a steel trap. These teeth give the killer whale a great advantage in hunting for food.

(7) Killer whales can be found in every ocean, but they are most often found where the water is very cold. They live with other whales in groups called pods. Each pod may have as little as two whales or as many as fifty whales traveling together. (8) A whale might stay with the same pod for its entire life.

The members of each pod are like a family. They look after each other in many ways. (9) They feel responsible for each other. When a new baby, called a calf, is born, other whales help the baby begin its new life. (10) Healthy whales take care of the sick or injured ones. The whole family works together to find food. (11) It appears they are not satisfied until each member has a full stomach.

(12) Whales in each pod seem to have fun together, too. They enjoy leaping high into the air and crashing down with a tremendous splash. (13) Scientists call this activity breaching. Spy hopping is when a whale sticks its head above water to take a quick look around. (14) Maybe spy hopping is the way killer whales play hide-and-seek with friends.

(15) Killer whales have a well-developed sense of hearing which keeps them aware of what is going on around them. (16) Unlike people, they can tell which direction a sound is coming from underwater.

(17) Killer whales make many different sounds that only other killer whales are able to understand. (18) The baby calf probably learns this whale "language" from its parents. When a killer whale is in trouble, it can send out a signal for help. (19) The other whales in the pod use their keen sense of hearing to determine how far they must travel to help the whale in distress. (20) Listening carefully, they seem to know just what direction to head for the rescue.

(21) Killer whales are probably able to survive in the oceans not only because of their speed and their sharp teeth, but also because of their intelligence and their strong ties to the other members of the pod.

DIRECTIONS Reread each numbered and underlined sentence in the article and decide whether it states a fact or opinion. Write *fact* or *opinion* on the numbered lines below.

1. _____   8. _____   15. _____

2. _____   9. _____   16. _____

3. _____   10. _____   17. _____

4. _____   11. _____   18. _____

5. _____   12. _____   19. _____

6. _____   13. _____   20. _____

7. _____   14. _____   21. _____

REMEMBER Facts can be proved, while opinions cannot be proved.

The Star-Spangled Banner

Most people enjoy music, whether by playing a musical instrument, listening to music, or singing. In this lesson, you will read about the birth of the national anthem of the United States, as you learn the difference between statements of fact and statements of opinion.

 ## KEYS to Fact and Opinion

Facts are statements that can be proven. Opinions are beliefs, and cannot be proven.

LEARN A fact can be checked to prove whether or not it is true. An opinion tells what someone believes. We cannot prove opinions right or wrong. People often feel differently about the same thing.

Some words help the reader recognize statements of opinion. Some of these words are *think, seem, believe, feel, might,* and *probably.*

EXAMPLE
1. A jazz band played at the music festival last summer. (fact)
2. Bill thinks that everyone should learn to play the piano. (opinion)

DIRECTIONS Read the paragraph. Decide if each numbered sentence is a fact or an opinion. Write your answers on the lines below the paragraph.

(1) No one knows exactly how old music is. (2) Some people think music started with singing. (3) Others believe it started when early man first beat on a drum. (4) We do know that people have enjoyed music for thousands of years.

(1) _____ (2) _____

(3) _____ (4) _____

Practice With Fact and Opinion

DIRECTIONS Read each sentence. If the sentence states a fact, write *F* on the line in front of the sentence. If the sentence is an opinion, write *O*.

_____ 1. Music for marching is exciting.

_____ 2. The violin is the hardest instrument to play.

_____ 3. The pipe organ is the largest musical instrument.

_____ 4. Thomas Edison invented the first phonograph.

_____ 5. People should listen to more classical music.

_____ 6. A person with long arms can play a trombone more easily than a person with short arms.

_____ 7. A flute sounds nicer than a trumpet.

DIRECTIONS Each of these sentences contains *both* a fact and an opinion. Read each sentence. Then underline the fact in the sentence.

1. Drums are part of the rhythm section of a band or orchestra, and drum solos are really great!

2. My sister cannot play the clarinet very well, even though she practices every day.

3. Some people play musical instruments and other people sing, but playing a musical instrument is a lot harder than singing.

4. The choir concert is tonight, and it's going to be terrific!

DIRECTIONS Read about how Francis Scott Key created a poem that has since become the national anthem of the United States.

On September 13, 1814, a young lawyer sailed down Chesapeake Bay. The United States was at war with Great Britain. The young lawyer was Francis Scott Key, and his mission was to obtain the release of a Maryland physician being held prisoner on an English warship. The doctor had been captured by the British during the burning of Washington, D.C., and Key believed it was unfair to hold the doctor prisoner.

Key was successful in his mission, but not before he had been taken prisoner himself. Just as he reached the warship, the British began firing on the Americans at Fort McHenry. Although he thought he would be safe hiding behind some cargo, Key was spotted by a British officer.

All during the night, Key watched bombs exploding over Fort McHenry. Since it was dark, he had no way of knowing how the battle was going. In the flashes of light from the bursting bombs, however, he could see the American flag waving. As long as the flag still waved, Key knew the battle had not been lost.

Shortly before daylight, the firing stopped. When "dawn's early light" showed that the "Stars and Stripes" was still flying, Key thought it was the most beautiful sight he had ever seen. He decided then and there to put his feelings into poetry and immediately wrote the first verse of what later became the national anthem.

Key was released from the British warship later that day. As he sailed back to Baltimore, he wrote more verses to his poem. It was published in a newspaper a few days later, and soon it was being sung to an old tune that the English had brought to the colonies. Within a few months, it was known as "The Star-spangled Banner."

Francis Scott Key's song did not become the United States national anthem for well over one hundred years after he wrote the words. Although it became very popular in the 1800s, many people felt it was too hard to sing to be a national anthem. In 1931, however, Congress declared that, musically difficult or not, "The Star-spangled Banner" was to be the official national anthem of the United States.

1. _____ Francis Scott Key was a lawyer during the war of 1812.

_____ Key believed it was unfair to hold the doctor prisoner.

_____ Key sailed down Chesapeake Bay in September, 1814.

2. _____ Key thought he would be safe if he hid behind some cargo.

_____ The British bombed the Americans at Fort McHenry.

_____ Key was taken prisoner on the British warship.

3. _____ It was still dark when the battle ended, and Key did not know which side had won.

_____ At "dawn's early light," Key saw the American flag still waving.

_____ Key felt that the "Stars and Stripes" was the most beautiful sight he had ever seen.

4. _____ Key's song became very popular in the 1800s.

_____ Key's song became the national anthem in 1931.

_____ Many people felt that Key's song was too hard to sing to be a national anthem.

REMEMBER Facts can be proved true or false, while opinions cannot be proved either right or wrong.

Ants for Dinner

Because of their name, it won't surprise you to learn that anteaters eat ants! They also eat termites and other soft-bodied insects. In fact, they may slurp up as many as 30,000 insects in one night! In this lesson, you will read about three kinds of anteaters as you learn about cause and effect relationships between events.

 ## KEYS to Cause and Effect

The reason something happens is the cause. The result, or what happens, is the effect.

LEARN   When we read, we think about what happens in a story and why it happens. When we think about these two things, we are thinking about cause and effect. The reason *why* something happens is called the *cause*. The *effect* is *what happens* as a result of the cause.

EXAMPLE   Anteaters can tear open insect nests because they have sharp claws.

"Anteaters can tear open insect nests" tells us the event, or what happens. When we ask ourselves why they can do this, the answer, "because they have sharp claws," tells us the cause.

DIRECTIONS   Read each sentence. Part of the sentence is underlined. Write *cause* or *effect* on the line in front of the sentence to describe the underlined group of words.

_____   **1.** Because ants are so small, <u>an anteater must eat many ants to get filled up.</u>

_____   **2.** Anteaters have sticky tongues, <u>so insects will stick to them.</u>

_____   **3.** Anteaters use their claws to fight <u>only when they are very frightened.</u>

② Practice With Cause and Effect

Draw a line from each cause in the list to its most probable effect.

CAUSE	EFFECT
1. I studied for three hours	and the cattle wandered into the road.
2. We played good defense	so the grass is really high.
3. The pasture gate blew open	and our coach is very pleased with us.
4. We've had nine days of rain	so I was prepared for the science test.

Read each sentence. On the lines below each sentence, write the cause and the effect. Don't forget that *the effect tells what happened* and *the cause tells why.*

1. The boy was surprised that his sloppy paper was given a good grade.

   Effect _____

   _____

   Cause _____

   _____

2. When part of the wing broke off, the plane began to veer wildly.

   Effect _____

   _____

   Cause _____

   _____

3. When the river reached flood stage, people had to abandon their homes.

   Effect _____

   _____

   Cause _____

   _____

4. With the invention of a new vaccine, the polio epidemic came to an end.

   Effect _____

   _____

   Cause _____

   _____

5. My cousin didn't use sun screen at the beach and got a bad sunburn.

   Effect _____

   _____

   Cause _____

   _____

3 Read and Apply

DIRECTIONS Read about three kinds of anteaters and some of their characteristics.

The long nose of the giant anteater of Central and South America is a very useful tool for probing into ant and termite nests. Shaped like a garden hose, that strange-looking nose also has an excellent sense of smell. It can sniff out ant and termite nests up to forty yards away.

The giant anteater does most of its hunting at night. It shuffles around with its nose to the ground. When it finds a nest, it rips a hole in it with its sharp claws and pokes its snout into the hole. Then, using another good piece of equipment—its long, sticky tongue—it slurps out hundreds of insects in a short time.

Ants and termites do not make it easy for the anteater. They not only bite and sting, but some of them spray unpleasant chemicals. A giant anteater does not stay at a nest very long. After about thirty seconds it goes off in search of another one. Sometimes it has to wander six miles or so in one night in order to get enough to eat.

There are two other species of anteaters, and both of these also live in Central and South America. One species is called the silky anteater, because of its soft, silky coat. The other is called the tamandua. Both these anteaters have shorter snouts than the giant anteater, and both are equipped with prehensile tails that help them hang from the branches of trees. The silky anteater always hunts for its food in trees, but the tamandua hunts both in trees and on the ground.

In addition to eating the same food, the three species of anteaters have another common characteristic—they have no teeth. Because of this, scientists have given them a "family" name of *Edentata*, which means "toothless." Since their diet consists of soft-bodied insects, having no teeth is not a disadvantage at all!

Using the article, match each cause with its effect by writing the letter of the effect on the line in front of the cause.

CAUSES

_____ **1.** Because it has a long nose and an excellent sense of smell,

_____ **2.** Because the giant anteater has a long, sticky tongue,

_____ **3.** Because ants and termites bite, sting, and spray chemicals,

_____ **4.** In order to get enough to eat,

_____ **5.** Because it has silky fur,

_____ **6.** Because they have prehensile tails,

_____ **7.** Because they are toothless,

_____ **8.** Because their diet consists of soft-bodied insects,

EFFECTS

a. a giant anteater does not stay at one nest very long.

b. scientists have given anteaters the family name of *Edentata,* which means "toothless."

c. silky anteaters and tamanduas can hang from tree branches.

d. a giant anteater can sniff out nests up to forty yards away.

e. anteaters do not need teeth.

f. one species of anteater is called the silky anteater.

g. it can slurp out hundreds of insects from a nest in a short time.

h. a giant anteater may have to wander six miles in one night.

REMEMBER An effect tells what happened. A cause tells why it happened.

108 Cause and Effect

Earthquakes

Imagine how frightening it would be to hear the earth start to rumble, to feel the ground move under your feet, and to see buildings swaying. These are some of the things that can happen during an earthquake. In this lesson, you will read about the causes of earthquakes and some kinds of damage that earthquakes produce. You will also learn about cause and effect relationships between events.

KEYS to Cause and Effect

Some events cause other events to happen.

LEARN When one thing happens, it can cause something else to happen. We call this a *cause and effect* relationship. When we think of *why* something happens, we are thinking about *cause.* When we think about *what happened,* we are thinking about *effect.*

EXAMPLE Many homes were damaged because the earthquake was so strong.

Ask yourself "What happened?" This will be the effect. The effect is that "many homes were damaged." Now ask yourself "Why were many homes damaged?" The answer, "because the earthquake was so strong," is the cause.

Signal words like *because, since, so,* and *that is why* tell us there is probably a cause and effect relationship between events.

DIRECTIONS Read each sentence. Draw one line under the cause and two lines under the effect in each sentence.

1. Because there is no warning, most people are surprised when an earthquake occurs.

2. Since they might be injured by falling objects, people stay indoors during an earthquake.

2 Practice With Cause and Effect

DIRECTIONS   Circle the word that tells if the underlined part of each sentence is the *cause* or the *effect*.

1. Because tall buildings can be <u>severely damaged by a strong earthquake</u>, some cities have passed laws that buildings can only be ten stories high.

    cause   effect

2. Long ago, some people believed earthquakes were caused by the <u>sudden movement of a mysterious power holding up the earth.</u>

    cause   effect

3. The state of California is sometimes <u>called "earthquake country"</u> since there have been so many earthquakes there.

    cause   effect

4. <u>Since the vast majority of earthquakes are very small</u>, most of them go undetected except by the most sensitive scientific instruments.

    cause   effect

5. Since the rumbling sound of an earthquake starts about thirty seconds before the quake itself, <u>the sound can't really be used as a warning signal.</u>

    cause   effect

6. Because "cracks" run all through the planet Earth, <u>earthquakes can happen anywhere in the world.</u>

    cause   effect

7. The vibrations of a mild earthquake <u>may cause dishes to rattle, pictures to fall off the wall, and floors to shake.</u>

    cause   effect

8. Scientists want to be able to predict when an earthquake will occur so <u>they can warn people in advance.</u>

    cause   effect

110 Cause and Effect

DIRECTIONS Read about earthquakes and why they happen.

Most scientists would agree that (1) an earthquake occurs (2) after the breaking or shifting of a huge mass of rock beneath the earth's surface. After the shift the rock bounces back into place. When this happens, large amounts of energy are released. (3) This energy is changed into vibrations (4) that shake the surrounding earth.

Usually earthquakes will occur in areas where there is a break, or fault, in the crust of the earth. (5) These faults appear (6) when a large mass of rock fractures and begins to separate in two different directions. The rock mass on one side of the crack may move up and down or to the left or right of the rock mass on the other side of the crack.

The movement in a large fault does not happen all at one time. It usually occurs little by little over a period of several thousand years. An earthquake is caused not by the slow movement of the fault, but by (7) a sudden shifting or cracking of part of the rock mass along the fault.

Major faults can be hundreds of miles long. In California, the San Andreas fault extends for about 600 miles. (8) When a portion of the rock along this fault suddenly broke loose near San Francisco in 1906, (9) it caused one of the greatest American earthquake disasters in history.

DIRECTIONS Reread the numbered and underlined phrases in the article. On the lines below, write *cause* or *effect* to describe each phrase.

1. _____   4. _____   7. _____

2. _____   5. _____   8. _____

3. _____   6. _____   9. _____

The side effects of earthquakes are often more destructive than the earthquake itself.

When an earthquake occurs on land, it is usually in a place that is dry and sandy. Here, long cracks called fissures may appear in the ground. These can be many feet wide. Sometimes the fissures close up within a few seconds, "swallowing" buildings.

Vibrations from earthquakes occurring in mountainous areas can cause tremendous landslides. Often the force of the debris that slides down the mountainside can be extremely destructive, even burying whole towns below.

Earthquakes that take place on the ocean floor, or on land near an ocean, can create huge waves of water known as *tsunamis*. These powerful waves travel up to 600 miles per hour. They can destroy lives and property as far as several thousand miles away from the source of the earthquake.

DIRECTIONS Complete the sentences with one of these three words:

landslides   fissures   tsunamis

1. Earthquakes occurring on dry, sandy land can cause _____.

2. The burying of towns under debris sliding down mountainsides is caused by

_____.

3. Earthquakes occurring under or near an ocean can cause _____.

4. Buildings can be "swallowed" by closing _____.

5. Destruction thousands of miles from an earthquake can be caused by a

_____.

REMEMBER Cause and effect relationships often exist between two events.

The Good Snake

Many people consider the cobra to be one of the most dangerous snakes in the world. It is true that cobra venom can cause death to humans, but it is also true that in some ways cobras actually help people. In this lesson, you will read about cobras and why some people in India call them the "good snake." You will also learn about cause and effect.

 ## KEYS to Cause and Effect

Why did it happen?

LEARN Young children learn by asking "Why?" They are trying to find out what caused something to happen.

EXAMPLE Many people dislike snakes because they are afraid of being bitten.

In this sentence, the effect is "many people dislike snakes." The *cause* of that effect is that "they are afraid of being bitten."

DIRECTIONS Read each sentence. Part of the sentence is underlined. Decide whether that part is a cause or effect and circle the correct word.

1. Because some cobras have two circular markings on their hoods, <u>some people mistakenly think these are its eyes.</u>

        cause   effect

2. The spitting cobra of Africa can cause great pain and temporary blindness <u>by squirting venom into its enemy's eyes.</u>

        cause   effect

2 Practice With Cause and Effect

DIRECTIONS There is a cause and effect relationship in each pair of sentences below. Write *C* in front of the sentence that describes the cause. Write *E* in front of the sentence that describes the effect.

1. _____ When rats and mice see a cobra, it is very likely the last thing they will ever see.

   _____ A cobra strikes and bites its prey very rapidly.

2. _____ Most snakes, including cobras, do not want to be near humans.

   _____ Cobras will usually slide away without a sound when they see a person.

3. _____ Snakes, like all reptiles, are cold-blooded.

   _____ A snake's skin feels cool and sometimes a little clammy.

4. _____ Many hunters and hikers carry snake-bite kits.

   _____ There is often the possibility of getting bitten by a snake when traveling through fields and woods.

5. _____ Scientists capture many snakes to study their habits.

   _____ Scientists have learned a great deal about the behavior of snakes.

6. _____ All snakes are deaf.

   _____ A cobra does not really hear the music of a snake charmer.

7. _____ It is not hard to find a cobra in India.

   _____ Cobras are plentiful in India's rice paddies and wheat fields.

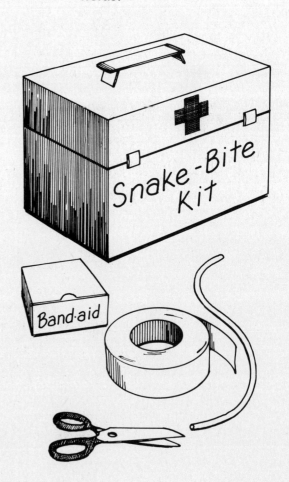

DIRECTIONS Read about cobras, and how they can be helpful to humans.

Cobras are found in both African and Asian countries. There are several species of cobra, the most well-known being the Egyptian cobra and the Indian cobra.

All cobras have hoods behind their necks that can be inflated or expanded. Their necks have flexible ribs that are capable of swinging outward. When this happens, the thin, loose skin of the cobra's neck is stretched, something like an umbrella being opened. A cobra raises the upper part of its body and expands its hood when it is excited or frightened. When it does this, distinctive markings on the hood are displayed. To some people, these markings resemble fierce-looking eyes.

Cobras eat rodents, frogs and toads, and birds. Some even eat other snakes. If food is scarce, they will eat large insects such as grasshoppers. A cobra strikes rapidly, biting its prey with short fangs. Then it hangs on while it injects its poisonous venom into the wound. The venom originates in glands located behind the cobra's eyes, and then runs down ducts to the fangs.

Cobras are usually feared by people because they do bite humans, and their venom can cause death. However, cobras don't go looking for people to bite and, like most snakes, they try to avoid humans if possible.

Actually, in some ways, cobras are more helpful than harmful. For one thing, scientists have learned how to use cobra venom in a pain-killing drug that is safer than many other drugs. Cobras also kill and eat millions of rats and mice in the countries in which they live. Rats and mice not only spread disease, but also eat crops. By killing these rodents, cobras help to protect humans from both disease and hunger. Recognizing this, some people in India have given the cobra the name "nulla pambu," meaning "good snake."

Read each sentence. Then draw one line under the cause and two lines under the effect.

1. A cobra can expand its hood because its neck has flexible ribs that can swing outward.

2. When a cobra becomes excited or frightened, it will expand its hood.

3. Because of their distinctive pattern, some people think the markings on a cobra's hood resemble fierce-looking eyes.

4. Cobras may eat large insects if their normal food supply becomes scarce.

5. Since cobras do bite humans and their venom can be fatal, many people are afraid of these snakes.

6. Cobras actually help humans because scientists have found a way to use cobra venom in a pain-killing drug.

7. Since cobras also kill rodents that spread disease and eat crops, they help protect people from disease and hunger.

8. Because it does help humans in some ways, some people in India have named the cobra ''nulla pambu,'' meaning ''good snake.''

REMEMBER Watch for a cause and effect relationship between two events.

116 Cause and Effect

Those Miserable Allergies

If you find yourself sneezing and blowing your nose, but you don't feel like you have a cold, you probably have an allergy. One of the most common allergies, hay fever, produces exactly these symptoms. In this lesson, you will read about allergies as you learn about cause and effect relationships.

KEYS to Cause and Effect

When an event is caused by another event, there is a cause and effect relationship between the two.

LEARN Things that happen are often a result of something else that happened first. The first event is called the *cause*. The result of that event is called the *effect*.

EXAMPLE Touching poison ivy causes many people to get itchy blisters on their skin.

In this sentence, "touching poison ivy" is the cause. What happens to many people as a result of touching poison ivy? They "get itchy blisters on their skin." This is the effect. The cause is not necessarily the first event to be mentioned in the sentence or passage.

DIRECTIONS Read each sentence. Then draw one line under the cause in the sentence, and draw two lines under the effect.

1. Some people get allergic reactions when they eat certain foods.

2. The first frost in the fall makes many of the plants that produce pollen die.

3. Because some people are very allergic to certain insect bites and stings, they protect their bodies by using a good insect repellent.

Practice With Cause and Effect

DIRECTIONS Match each cause and effect by writing the correct letter on the line.

_____ 1. People who have a lot of allergies

_____ 2. Some people cannot be around dogs or cats

_____ 3. Allergies

_____ 4. Children often outgrow food allergies

_____ 5. The tendency to have allergies seems to run in families

_____ 6. Installing an air conditioner or air filter in your home

a. cause the same symptoms as many illnesses.

b. so if your parents are allergic to things, chances are that you will be also.

c. because they are allergic to furry animals.

d. can help you if you are allergic to dust.

e. may feel miserable until they get medical help.

f. and can then eat the foods that used to give them problems.

DIRECTIONS Complete these two sentences by writing a cause for the first one and an effect for the second.

1. I get upset when _____

_____ .

2. I didn't do my homework so _____

_____ .

3 Read and Apply

DIRECTIONS Read about some common causes of allergies.

If you are constantly sneezing, blowing your nose, and rubbing your itchy, watery eyes, you may have hay fever. Hay fever is an allergy that has been misnamed, for it is caused by pollen from flowers, not by hay. For most people, hay fever season begins in late summer and continues into the fall. At this time of year, the wind moves a lot of pollen through the air. After the first frost in the area kills the ragweed and other plants that give off pollen, hay fever sufferers can finally breathe freely again!

Other things besides pollen cause allergic reactions in people. Dust, molds, and feathers are "high-allergy" items. So are pets, particularly furry and feathered ones. Some people are allergic to certain food. Others are allergic to some medicine. Eating food and taking medicine to which they are allergic can cause people to develop stomach aches, rashes, hives, or even a fever.

Finally, things that people touch can cause itchy rashes in allergic persons. One big offender, of course, is poison ivy. Others are soaps and lotions.

DIRECTIONS Some of the items in the list below are common causes of allergies. Others are common reactions, or effects. If the item is a cause of an allergy, write C on the line. If it is an effect, write E.

_____ medicine   _____ runny nose   _____ sneezing   _____ pollen

_____ hives   _____ dust   _____ rashes   _____ food

_____ pets   _____ itchy eyes   _____ poison ivy   _____ fever

_____ feathers   _____ stomach aches   _____ molds   _____ soap

Cause and Effect **119**

Many of the symptoms of allergic reactions are familiar to you. They are the same symptoms you have when you are sick. (1) <u>Colds and flu viruses</u>, for instance, usually cause sneezing and runny noses, and sometimes stomach aches and fevers. Other viruses, such as measles and chicken pox, cause rashes. These symptoms (2) <u>are a result of your body declaring war on outside invaders.</u> When bacteria and viruses enter your body, they cause it (3) <u>to produce chemicals called antibodies to fight off the invaders. These antibodies travel through the bloodstream to destroy the</u> germs. Runny noses, watery eyes, and sneezing are all part of the battle.

People with allergies have protective systems that seem to go overboard; (4) <u>even relatively harmless things such as pollen or dust are treated as "hostile aliens."</u> Then the sneezing and nose-blowing starts. An allergic person can get help, however, from the medical profession. Specially trained allergy doctors can help track down the specific allergies a person has. (5) <u>Then the doctor can prescribe medication or give shots</u> (6) <u>so the allergy sufferer can get relief.</u>

DIRECTIONS Write the word *cause* or *effect* on the lines to describe the numbered and underlined groups of words in the article.

1. _____   4. _____

2. _____   5. _____

3. _____   6. _____

REMEMBER Understanding cause and effect relationships helps you understand what you read.

Four Marsupials

By the time you started school, you already knew a lot. You knew the difference between animals and birds and between adults and children. You learned by comparing and contrasting. In this lesson, you will learn more about comparing and contrasting as you read about four marsupials of Australia and New Guinea.

 1 KEYS to Comparing and Contrasting

Look for likenesses and differences when you compare and contrast.

LEARN People compare and contrast many types of things. You might compare different people, different types of jobs, or different types of houses. When comparing things, look for likenesses or differences, or both.

EXAMPLE Roses are red and violets are blue,
Sugar is sweet and so are you.

The first line of this rhyme contrasts two flowers by telling the difference in their colors. The second lines compares ''you'' and sugar—you both are sweet!

DIRECTIONS Compare the things in each group. Circle the words that name the things that are most alike. Then draw a box around the one thing that is most different from the other three. The first one is done for you.

1. chickens	cardinals	squirrels	robins
2. ladder	bed	cot	chair
3. scissors	pen	crayon	pencil
4. physicians	surgeons	nurses	pilots
5. grass	rocks	trees	shrubs

② Practice Comparing and Contrasting

LEARN   One way to compare and contrast different things is to make an analogy. For example, we can say "Boots are to feet as mittens are to hands." In this analogy, <u>boots</u> and <u>mittens</u> are both articles of clothing, and <u>feet</u> and <u>hands</u> are both parts of the body. The analogy shows that a difference between boots and mittens is where they are worn.

DIRECTIONS   Use the words in the box to complete each analogy. Write the correct word on the line. The first one has been done for you.

hospital	barn	pencil	night
clothes	vegetables	glasses	elephant
ears	sails	cooks	skis

1. Lead is to __pencil__ as ink is to pen.

2. Snake is to reptile as _____ is to mammal.

3. Rings are to fingers as earrings are to _____.

4. Cups are to coffee as _____ are to iced tea.

5. _____ are to skiers as racquets are to tennis players.

6. Doctor is to _____ as judge is to courtroom.

7. Skyscraper is to cities as _____ is to country.

8. Tools are to handymen as utensils are to
_____.

9. _____ are to humans as fur is to animals.

10. Bananas are to fruit as peas are to
_____.

11. _____ are to sailboats as paddles are to canoes.

12. Dark is to _____ as light is to day.

Read and Apply

DIRECTIONS Read about four marsupials of Australia and New Guinea. Look for likenesses and differences between the animals.

What do kangaroos, koalas, wombats, and bandicoots all have in common? They are all marsupials, and all are found only in Australia or nearby New Guinea.

A marsupial is a mammal, but while most mammals give birth to well-developed young, the marsupials do not. Their young are very immature when born and must continue to develop for several months in a pouch located outside the mother's body.

Kangaroos are the largest of the Australian marsupials. There are five species of larger kangaroos and about forty species of smaller kangaroos. Most species have large, powerful hind legs, short front legs, and a long tail. They travel by hopping on their hind legs, using their tails for balance. The larger kangaroos, called great kangaroos, can travel up to forty miles per hour and can jump over objects as high as six feet. Kangaroos are plant-eaters, feeding mostly on grasses.

Koalas are also plant-eating marsupials. A koala—which looks like a Teddy bear but is not a bear at all—feeds mostly on eucalyptus leaves and shoots. In fact, a koala spends most of its life in eucalyptus trees, even sleeping in them in the daytime. The word *koala* is an Australian aborigine word meaning "no drink." Koalas in the wild do not drink water, but get the liquid they need from eucalyptus leaves.

Two burrowing marsupials are the wombat and the bandicoot. Wombats are much larger than bandicoots. A wombat may be up to four feet long and weigh from thirty to seventy-five pounds. Bandicoots, which look something like rats, are small and most weigh less than two pounds. Wombats and bandicoots also have different diets. Wombats are plant-eaters, feeding on grass, leaves and roots, while bandicoots eat insects, spiders and worms.

DIRECTIONS Use the article to answer the questions.

1. What three marsupials are alike because they all eat plants?

_____

_____

_____

2. What two marsupials are alike because they both eat grasses?

_____

_____

3. What marsupial is different because it is a meat-eater?

_____

4. Compare the wombat and the bandicoot by telling one way they are alike and two ways in which they are different.

Alike: _____

_____

Different: _____

_____

_____

_____

5. How are kangaroos and koalas different with respect to what they eat?

_____

_____

_____

6. In what ways are koalas, kangaroos, bandicoots, and wombats alike?

_____

_____

_____

7. How does a marsupial differ from most other mammals?

_____

_____

_____

_____

_____

_____

_____

REMEMBER Things or ideas can be compared and contrasted by showing how they are alike and how they are different.

Jumping Firefighters!

How do firefighters reach fires where there are no roads? In this lesson, you'll read about firefighters from the sky as you learn about words that do not always mean what they say.

KEYS to Figurative Language

Figures of speech don't mean what they say.

LEARN *Figures of speech* are words that are used to mean something other than what they say. Figurative language helps you see a picture in your mind. It also makes your reading more interesting.

EXAMPLE She was on cloud nine when she passed all the tests.
My little sister is a pain in the neck.

The phrase *on cloud nine* means *extremely happy*. A *pain in the neck* is a figurative way of saying she's *a bother*.

DIRECTIONS Underline the figure of speech in each sentence.

1. You'll be in hot water if Mom finds out you broke the window.

2. When we came to the fork in the road, we didn't know which way to go.

3. I can't answer the phone, because I'm tied up at the moment.

4. My dad got home just in the nick of time.

5. It's raining cats and dogs out there!

Practice With Figurative Language

2

DIRECTIONS Read each sentence. Find the real meaning of the underlined words in the list below. Write the meaning on the line.

1. During their difficult training, smokejumpers might think about throwing in the towel.

   _____

2. A forest fire is nothing to sneeze at.

   _____

3. The fact that she was one of the first female smokejumpers is a real feather in her cap.

   _____

4. The captain told the reporters to hold their horses.

   _____

5. Smokejumpers work to beat the band to keep a fire from spreading.

   _____

6. When the wind is blowing hard, smokejumpers know there are rough waters ahead.

   _____

7. Smokejumpers know a forest fire will not just blow over.

   _____

8. At times, smokejumpers would surely give their eyeteeth for some rest.

   _____

a. high honor
b. give anything, wish for
c. slow down
d. be gone shortly

e. long and hard
f. hard times
g. quitting
h. not a small thing

126 Figurative Language

3

Read and Apply

Look for figures of speech as you read the story.

An ear piercing howl filled the air. Wendy jumped at the sound. Then she stopped dead in her tracks as she heard a voice on the loudspeaker call, ''Fire in the Bitterroot Forest!''

As she ran to the equipment room, Wendy could hear the airplane engines roaring. Keeping in mind that the plane would be in the air in three minutes, she pulled on her padded jumpsuit as quick as a wink. Remaining calm, as she'd been trained to do, she buckled the 35-pound parachute pack onto her back. With her helmet under her arm, she scurried to the plane. Seconds later, the plane was in the air.

The smokejumpers had a bird's-eye view of the forest from the plane.

''There it is!'' shouted one of Wendy's teammates.

In the canyon below, they saw that the wind was already pushing the fire from tree to tree. The smokejumpers moved around their supplies to form a line at the front of the plane. Now all eyes were on the spotter, whose job it was to weigh all the facts and tell each firefighter when to jump. Wendy stood at the door, ready for her turn.

As soon as they hit the ground, the smokejumpers collected their parachutes and other gear in a flash. Looking upward, they spotted their supplies of tools, food, and drinking water being dropped.

''Let's work our way forward!'' yelled the lead smokejumper. ''No matter what happens, remember to keep your head!''

Read to find the meaning of the underlined figure of speech. Circle the letter of the correct answer.

1. The phrase <u>keep your head</u> means
   a. think about what you are doing.
   b. put your head down.
   c. make sure that you don't bump your head.

2. Smokejumpers land beside or in back of a fire to keep from being <u>backed into a corner</u>. This means
   a. having your back hurt in a corner.
   b. being pushed into a corner of the woods.
   c. being trapped in the middle of a fire.

3. Smokejumpers <u>lend a hand</u> during a fire. This means
   a. they give one of their hands.
   b. they give their help.
   c. they loan their money.

4. When firefighters <u>hit the ground</u>, they
   a. land on the ground.
   b. stomp on the ground with their boots.
   c. win the right to jump next.

5. When <u>all eyes are on the spotter</u>, the smokefighters
   a. give their eyes to the spotter.
   b. keep watching the spotter.
   c. are afraid of the spotter.

6. The spotter who <u>weighs all the facts</u> must
   a. watch all events and make good decisions.
   b. put all the facts on a scale to find their weight.
   c. know each firefighter's weight and height.

REMEMBER A figure of speech helps you picture what is happening.

Just a Matter of Time

Does time seem to stand still when you're bored? Does it seem to fly when you're having fun? In this lesson, you'll read about a time in your life that sometimes seemed endless to your parents but actually flew by all too quickly. You'll also learn about groups of words that present interesting images.

 ## 1 KEYS to Figurative Language

Some words and phrases create vivid images.

LEARN A *figure of speech* is a group of words that suggests one thing but means another. The *literal* meaning of the words is their true meaning, while the *figurative* meaning is how they create a sharp picture in your mind. The context, or the rest of the words, helps you understand figurative language. One kind of figure of speech is an *idiom*.

EXAMPLE Nora felt her mom's opinion of clothes was *behind the times*.

Literally speaking, Nora's mom's opinion is hidden by some clocks, but that doesn't make sense. The figurative meaning of the idiom tells us that Nora thinks her mom's opinion is old-fashioned.

DIRECTIONS Read each sentence and underline the idiom. Then write *L* for literal or *F* for figurative before each meaning.

1. Neil needed to buy time, so he asked for a later deadline.

    _____ **a.** purchase a watch or clock

    _____ **b.** get more hours, days, or weeks

2. Maria rounded the corner just in the nick of time.

    _____ **a.** on top of a chipped area of the clock

    _____ **b.** at the very last minute

(2) Practice With Figurative Language

DIRECTIONS Two often-used figures of speech are the *simile* and the *metaphor*. Both kinds of figurative language use a word or phrase to show a likeness between two things. A simile uses the words *like* or *as,* while a metaphor does not.

Simile: Kristen ran like a scared puppy.

Metaphors: The ship plowed the waves.

The simile uses *like* to compare Kristen's quickness with that of a frightened puppy. The metaphor tells how a vessel moving through the water is like a plow moving through earth. Read each sentence. Write *simile* or *metaphor* on line *a.* Then write the two things being compared on line *b.* The first one is done for you.

1. The screaming car woke me from a deep sleep.

   a. metaphor

   b. person's loud yell _____ and car's loud noise _____

2. Monica slept as peacefully as a baby through all the commotion.

   a. _____

   b. _____ and _____

3. That clock's chimes are like sirens if you're trying to sleep.

   a. _____

   b. _____ and _____

4. Jonathan is as graceful as a fish in the water.

   a. _____

   b. _____ and _____

5. My mom is convinced that my stomach is a bottomless pit.

   a. _____

   b. _____ and _____

6. The baseball came over the plate like a heat-seeking missile.

   a. _____

   b. _____ and _____

Read and Apply

Look for figurative language as you read about the earliest time of your life.

When you were born, your birth time was recorded by the hour, minute, month, day, and year. A clock was consulted each time you ate, slept, and woke. Your life was recorded in time as your age was told in hours, days, months, and finally, years.

Your parents were confident that you'd sleep through the night all in good time. For the time being though, they walked around like zombies from lack of restful sleep. Your parents, who had once had time on their hands, now seemed to be racing against time. The job of parenting, they found, was no part-time occupation. They always seemed to run out of time and were forever working overtime. As they watched you bloom, however, they wished time would stand still. You were continually exploding into a new stage of development, and they loved spending time with you and watching the fruits of their labors.

Time flew, and soon you were like a locomotive chugging through the house on all fours as fast as lightning. Now your parents knew there were tough times ahead. It was just a matter of time before your curiosity would attack with both barrels. No plant or precious collectible would be safe. Time and time again, they snatched you from the jaws of danger. Finally, figuring a stitch in time would save nine, they put away fragile things, cleared the house of poisonous plants, padlocked the cupboards, and placed other potential dangers out of your reach.

When you'd had it with caterpillar creeping, you began to have the time of your life teetering like a newborn calf. You made your parents' day when you took those first steps. They were there with a camera as quick as a flash to capture the moment. You seemed to be making up for lost time as you raced like a thoroughbred through every hour of the day. There was no stopping you, once you had your wings!

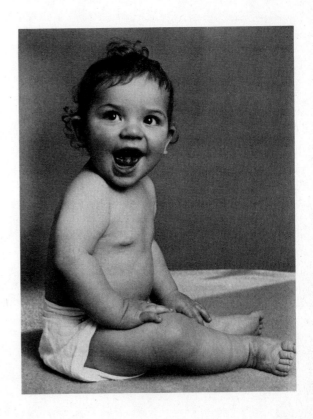

Read each idiom used in the article you just read. Choose the phrase's meaning from the box. Write the meaning on the line.

over and over	eventually
having fun	extra time
being too busy	gave joy
going fast	do now as prevention

1. racing against time _____

2. the time of your life _____

3. a stitch in time would save nine _____

4. time on their hands _____

5. time and time again _____

6. made your parents' day _____

7. making up for lost time _____

8. all in good time _____

DIRECTIONS Find each of the similes and metaphors in the article you read. On the lines write the two things being compared.

1. you had your wings _____ _____

2. watched you bloom _____ _____

3. as fast as lightning _____ _____

4. continually exploding _____ _____

5. like a thoroughbred _____ _____

6. attack with both barrels _____ _____

7. like a newborn calf _____ _____

8. like a locomotive _____ _____

REMEMBER Use context to get the meaning of figurative language.

Reading Between the Lines

Sometimes authors write with the purpose of influencing your thinking one way or another. In this lesson, you'll learn to recognize words and phrases that were written to sway the reader. You'll learn to recognize clues that signal a need to "read between the lines."

 ## KEYS to Bias

A writer may have a strong point of view.

LEARN A *bias* is a strong opinion or judgment which is not easily affected by facts or new experiences. A person expresses a bias by using words which are meant to sway the reader to a particular way of thinking. Recognizing the existence of bias helps a reader to interpret what is read.

Park Opens At Rushville
Rushville Park Finally Opens
Yet Another Park In Rushville

The first newspaper headline states a fact with no biased attempt to sway the reader. In the second, the use of the word *finally* shows that the author thinks the park should have opened long ago. The author of the third headline feels strongly that Rushville now has too many parks.

DIRECTIONS Read each statement. Write *bias* or *no bias* on the line to tell about the feeling behind the words.

1. It's time someone questioned this old-fashioned rule. _____

2. The schools are gearing up to begin a new year. _____

3. We feel this is a monumental injustice and must not be tolerated any

    longer. _____

4. My music teacher just assigned a new lesson. _____

2 Practice Recognizing Bias

DIRECTIONS Bias is sometimes disguised. One sentence alone may not show bias, but it may support other biased sentences around it. Words that are judgmental are often clues that the writer has a bias in favor of, or against, something. A short person might be described as a "shrimp" or "runt" from a biased viewpoint. Advertising uses bias in an attempt to have readers believe in a product and purchase it. Television and newspaper editorials are often presented from a biased viewpoint.

Read each statement. Then read the interpretation of the statement and circle the correct word in parentheses. Write the key words or phrases that help you recognize the bias in the statement. The first one is done for you.

1. We simply cannot allow this sinister activity in our community.

   A. The author   (favors /(opposes)   a particular activity.

   B. Key words: _simply cannot allow, sinister_

2. There can't be a better candidate for the office than this hard-working patriot.

   A. The writer   (would / would not)   like to see the candidate elected.

   B. Key words: _____

3. Kids are undoubtedly the best judges of what's fair in this situation.

   A. Kids are being   (supported / opposed)   by the writer.

   B. Key words: _____

4. Anyone who rides without a seat belt is playing with fire.

   A. The use of seat belts is   (favored / opposed) .

   B. Key words: _____

5. Marty sat there chewing on his nails and looking downright ridiculous.

   A. The observer   (is / is not)   impressed by Marty's actions.

   B. Key words: _____

3 Read and Apply

DIRECTIONS Look for bias as you read the opposing editorials.

A. The Olympic Committee simply must take skateboarding seriously. Skateboarding should be carefully considered for inclusion in the Olympic Games. The popular sport certainly deserves respect and honor as a sport that's here to stay. A favorite of the young and agile since its discovery in the late 1950s in California, skateboarding reveals the incredible creativity and skill of today's youth. Like other Olympic sports, skateboarding requires split-second timing to perform endovers, wheelies, ollies, leg launches, and various other maneuvers.

The legitimacy of skateboarding has already been recognized by many cities that have erected special parks and rinks for the board-skaters. Anywhere you turn, you can see amateurs and professionals competing. It's time, indeed, for skateboarding to be elevated to its proper rank as a major competitive sport.

B. The last thing we need is to turn on our television and see wildly-dressed youths skateboarding in Olympic competition. Surely no one would seriously suggest that this fad be taken so seriously. This sport, if you can call it that, is undoubtedly here today and gone tomorrow.

Everybody, young and old, enjoys watching the flawless routine of a gymnast, the rhythmic backstroke of a swimmer, the sleek, graceful movements of downhill skiers. How can skateboarding's aerial maneuvers tagged the "ollie," the "airwalk," or "hand plant" possibly be equated with our dignified sporting events?

The Olympics has worked hard for its fine reputation. The inclusion of a flash-in-the-pan sport like skateboarding would surely require us all to sit back and reevaluate our loyalties.

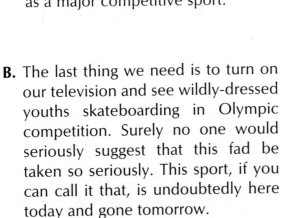

Recognizing Bias **135**

1. Find two phrases that tell you the author of Editorial B feels strongly that skateboarding will not be a lasting sport?

   _____

   _____

2. What word does the author of Editorial A use in an attempt to sway the reader to believe that skateboarding youths are creative and skillful?

   _____

3. What word is used in Editorial B to give the idea that skateboarders dress differently from the reader?

   _____

4. What two occurrences are cited as proof that skateboarding should be considered a legitimate sport of Olympic worth?

   _____

   _____

   _____

   _____

   _____

5. What word does Editorial B use to describe sports that are currently included in the Olympics?

   _____

DIRECTIONS Mark an X on the line before each statement that, when read alone, shows bias.

_____ 1. Many cities have erected parks and rinks for board-skaters.

_____ 2. The inclusion of a faddish sport like skateboarding would require us all to reevaluate our loyalties.

_____ 3. Skateboarding requires split-second timing.

_____ 4. Skateboarding had its beginning in the late 1950s in California.

_____ 5. These skateboarders dress in wild clothes and therefore must not be taken seriously.

_____ 6. The popular and lively sport of skateboarding deserves some honor and respect.

_____ 7. Skateboarders use special launch ramps.

_____ 8. The last thing we need is to have skateboarders entered in the Olympic Games.

_____ 9. Skateboarding is enjoyed by youths.

_____ 10. Some call skateboarding a sport, but it's really just playing with a toy.

REMEMBER Bias can be obvious or well-disguised.

A Talented American

You learned to speak in sentences, and later, you learned to read in sentences. In this lesson, you'll learn about the structure of sentences as you read about a talented American woman.

 ## KEYS to Grammar

A sentence is a group of words that expresses a complete thought.

LEARN   A sentence has a *subject* and a *predicate*. The subject tells who or what is being talked about. The predicate tells about the subject. Understanding sentence structure can help you understand long sentences.

Subject—Who or What?	*Predicate*—What about it?
Jill	laughed.
Brenda and Patrick	worked on the float.

EXAMPLE   Each subject names who is being talked about, while each predicate tells something about its subject.

DIRECTIONS   Read each sentence. Then write its subject and predicate under the correct headings.

1. Mary, Alice, and Becky are good friends.
2. Your dad will be here at 5:00.
3. That crying toddler over there is my brother.

Subject	Predicate
1. _____	_____ .
2. _____	_____ .
3. _____	_____ .

② Practice With Grammar

DIRECTIONS Read the paragraph. Then write each sentence on a line. Draw a line to separate the subject and the predicate. The first one is done for you.

Pat was nervous. Donnie was sitting near her. The girl from the other school was there. The large auditorium was crowded with people. The speaker received the slip of paper. The regional winners would now be announced.

1. Pat / was nervous.

2. _____

3. _____

4. _____

5. _____

6. _____

DIRECTIONS Combine the subjects and predicates to write six different sentences on the lines below. Each sentence must make sense.

Subjects	**Predicates**
The small dog	is leading the group.
Those people	stood near the bus.
A woman in glasses	buried a bone in our yard.

1. _____

2. _____

3. _____

4. _____

5. _____

6. _____

DIRECTIONS Read about a famous American painter who continued to work long after the age when most people retire.

By the 1920s, Georgia O'Keefe was well-known for her paintings of nature. Although some of her work is abstract art, or art that does not resemble particular things, the artist is best known for her canvas creations of things in nature such as flowers, rocks, and animal bones. One bloom would cover a whole canvas. An animal skull or a desert rock was often the subject of her work.

As a young woman in her thirties, Ms. O'Keefe had the honor of selling one of her paintings for more money than had ever been earned before by a living American artist. While this was amazing for such a young woman, it was only the beginning of a long record of successes.

Georgia O'Keefe, born in Sun Prairie, Wisconsin in 1887, studied at the Art Institute of Chicago, Columbia University, and other schools. While teaching at West Texas State University, Ms. O'Keefe had her first public exhibit in New York City in 1916.

After residing in New York City for several years, the artist moved to New Mexico in the 1930s. Here the beauty of the desert inspired more creations. The dry, arid land and red stones of the area excited her. The tan, red, and brown colors of the landscape became part of her paintings. One of Ms. O'Keefe's most striking paintings is of the skull of a longhorn steer. The painting, completed in 1936, shows a skull, clouds above mountain peaks, and lovely flowers.

Many people in their seventies and eighties are retired from their life's work. This was not true for Georgia O'Keefe who continued to create works of art until her death in 1986 at the age of 97. In her last years, she not only continued to paint, but also traveled about, teaching and sharing her knowledge with young artists.

Read each sentence. Mark an *X* in the proper column to tell if the underlined words are the subject or predicate.

	Subject	Predicate
1. Georgia O'Keefe was a famous American painter.	___	___
2. <u>Ms. O'Keefe</u> painted things in nature.	___	___
3. <u>The painting, completed in 1936,</u> showed a skull.	___	___
4. <u>Many people in their later years</u> retire.	___	___
5. Ms. O'Keefe <u>sold a painting for a record amount.</u>	___	___
6. The artist <u>studied at Columbia.</u>	___	___
7. <u>Georgia O'Keefe</u> painted until her death.	___	___
8. <u>The artist</u> enjoyed a long life of successes.	___	___
9. <u>Ms. O'Keefe, a teacher,</u> shared her knowledge.	___	___
10. One bloom <u>would cover a whole canvas.</u>	___	___

DIRECTIONS Read each sentence part. Write *subject* or *predicate* on the line.

_____ 1. the young man

_____ 2. will perhaps be known someday

_____ 3. these things in the basket

_____ 4. painted a picture of his animals

_____ 5. is all about skateboarding

_____ 6. my grandmother

_____ 7. he and his friends

_____ 8. formed a study group

_____ 9. don't belong to anyone in my class

_____ 10. wanted me to spend the summer

_____ 11. this book I'm holding

_____ 12. the group I just heard

REMEMBER Understanding subjects and predicates can help you understand long sentences.

Memory Tips

In this lesson, you'll learn some tips that will help you remember information you never want to forget.

 ## KEYS to Memory

Mnemonic devices are tips to jog your memory.

LEARN *Mnemonic devices* are helpful in remembering important lists, the spellings and meanings of words, or other information. Memory tips are usually sentences, phrases, or rhymes, but any kind of comparison or reference that helps you remember something is a mnemonic device.

EXAMPLE You want to remember the directions of the compass, so you picture the map of the United States and think:

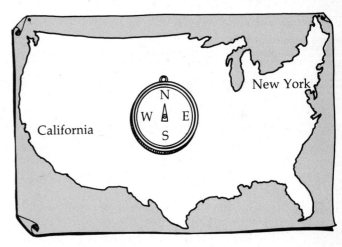

North is up; New York is *east.*
South is down, California is *west.*

DIRECTIONS Write how each sentence can help you remember a word's spelling.

1. There's a dollar sign in *expense.* _____

_____

2. One should never be*lie*ve a *lie.* _____

_____

② Practice With Memory

DIRECTIONS Read each paragraph and complete the sentences.

1. Mnemonic devices are often written in rhyme. This poem is helpful in spelling words with *ie* or *ei*.

   I before *e*
   Except after *c*,
   Or when sounded like *a*
   As in *neighbor* or *weigh*.

   Then there is *seizure*,
   And *weird*, also *leisure*,
   Fahrenheit, neither,
   Forfeit, height, either.

   a. I will usually write the letter _____ before the letter _____, unless the double vowel has the long sound of *a*.

   b. Eight words that are exceptions to the rule are:

   _____ _____ _____ _____

   _____ _____ _____ _____

2. To distinguish a bactrian camel from a dromedary camel, lay the first letter of the word for each kind of camel flat on its stick.

   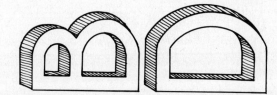

   a. How many humps does a dromedary camel have? _____

   b. How many humps are on a bactrian camel? _____

3. Do you sometimes forget how to divide fractions? Remember this rhyme and you'll never forget.

   The number you're dividing by,
   Turn upside down and multiply.

   a. To divide $^4/_7$ by $^1/_2$, you'd change $^1/_2$ to _____ and then multiply.

   b. In $^2/_9 \div {^4/_5}$, you'd turn _____ upside down before multiplying.

4. To remember that the divisor is the number on the outside of a division box, think of the divi*sor* knocking on the dividend's d*oor*.

   a. In $162\overline{)2{,}963}$, the divisor is _____ .

   b. When a dividend of 72,801 is divided by a divisor of 876, _____ is on the outside of the division box.

3 Read and Apply

DIRECTIONS Read the poem for remembering the parts of speech. Then complete the work below.

The Parts of Speech

Three little words you often see
Are *articles:* a, an, and the.
A *noun's* the name of anything—
As, garden or school, hoop or swing.
Adjectives tell the kind of noun—
As great, small, pretty, white, or brown.
Instead of nouns the *pronouns* stand:
Her head, his face, your arm, his hand.
Verbs tell of something being done:
To read, count, sing, laugh, jump, or run.

How things are done the *adverbs* tell—
As slowly, quickly, ill, or well.
Conjunctions join the words together—
As men and women, wind or weather.
The *preposition* stands before
A noun—as in or through a door.
The *interjection* shows surprise—
As oh! how pretty! ah! how wise!
The whole are called nine parts of speech
Which reading, writing, speaking teach.

—Michele Slung

1. Write the articles of speech. _____

2. *Expertly, quickly, beautifully,* and *well* are _____ .

3. *In, under, over,* and *through* are _____ .

4. *His, your, myself,* and *ourselves* are _____ .

DIRECTIONS Use a word in the word box to complete each rhyming mnemonic device.

1. Freshman, sophomore,

   Then a junior.

   Upon graduation,

   No longer a _____ .

2. If you lock the door before leaving the site.

   Your home is less likely a burglar's _____ .

3. When adding an *s*, *occur* has one *r*,

   But with other suffixes, *occur* gets bizarre.

   Two *r*'s in *occurrence, occurring, occurred;*

   No question! Mnemonics can help with this _____ .

4. When writing "it's,"

   Try "it is;" if it fits,

   Add apostrophe *s*.

   Then call it _____ .

5. Is it "Amy and I" or "Amy and me"?

   By leaving out "Amy," it's easy to see.

   The word that sounds best in this simple test

   Is the word that I'll use, and then add the _____ .

delight
senior
rest
word
quits

DIRECTIONS Think about the underlined clues as you answer the questions.

1. If you think of *him* as Franc*is* and *her* as Franc*es*, how might you remember the correct spelling for the male and female names?

   _____

   _____

   _____

2. What clue is in the word *perimeter* that helps you remember it is the distance around a figure?

   _____

REMEMBER Learn or create a mnemonic device to remember things.

Wordless Stories

How can a story be told without words? In this lesson, you'll learn about word-less stories you encounter in reading.

 KEYS to Picture Interpretation

Pictures add interest and help you understand ideas.

LEARN Pictures tell stories and give information. A caption under a picture can summarize the idea of the picture.

DIRECTIONS Study Ellen Janes Jon-tzen's painting. Then complete the sentences.

Concert in the Park

1. The reason the people in this picture

   are gathered together is _____

   _____

2. I know that the setting for this picture is a park because of the _____

   _____ in the picture and a word in the _____.

3. Some clues that this event takes place in the summer are

   a. _____

   b. _____

Practice Picture Interpretation

DIRECTIONS When a picture appears without a caption, the reader's job is to find clues in the picture to understand the artist's message. Study each picture. Then answer the questions below.

1. How does the girl on the right feel?

   _____

2. How does the girl on the left feel?

   _____

3. Why are the girls' backs to each other?

   _____

   _____

4. What might have happened prior to this picture? _____

   _____

1. What must have happened just prior to this picture?

   _____

2. How do you know the children did some planning before going after the dog?

   _____

   _____

3. How do you know the dog belongs to the children?

   _____

4. What does the dog apparently want to do?

   _____

DIRECTIONS   Read some reasons for the use of pictures. Then study each picture and answer the questions below.

To add a bit of humor.
To make written ideas more interesting or less difficult.
To express an idea that would otherwise require many words.

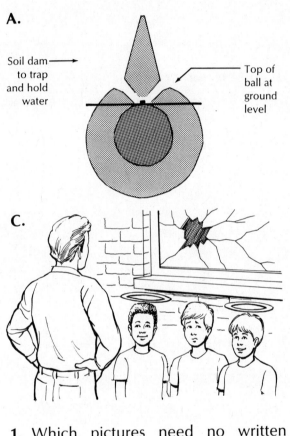

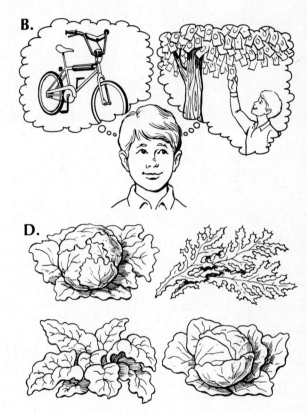

1. Which pictures need no written explanation for the reader to understand the message?

   _____

2. Which picture could help you differentiate between similar vegetables?

   _____

3. Which pictures might make you laugh?

   _____

4. Which picture might illustrate an article about how to do something properly?

   _____

5. Which pictures could make an article more interesting and new information easier to understand?

   _____

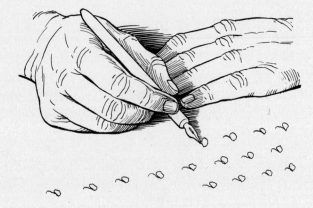

1. The term *financially embarrassed* means

   a. asked to purchase something you don't really want.

   b. having no money to buy what you want.

   c. feeling shy in the presence of an adult.

   d. wishing someone wouldn't laugh at you.

2. I know the meaning of *financially embarrassed* because the picture shows

   _____

   _____

   _____

3. I know this picture is of a time long ago because

   _____

   _____

   _____

1. The person in this picture

   a. is a young child learning penmanship.

   b. is a senior citizen who's probably a male.

   c. finds writing to be a very easy task.

2. A clue to the age of the person in this picture is

   _____

   _____

   _____

3. I can tell that this person is struggling to accomplish a task because

   _____

   _____

   _____

4. Which emotions does the artist hope the viewer will feel?

   a. appreciation and respect

   b. joy and helplessness

   c. sorrow and fear

REMEMBER Pictures tell wordless stories.

Graphically Speaking

Why do newspapers, books, and magazines have pictures, graphs, diagrams, or other drawings? In this lesson, you'll learn about the helpful overview graphic aids offer.

 KEYS to Graphic Aids

A graphic aid gives a quick overview of important data.

LEARN A graphic aid is any picture that helps you understand information. Charts, graphs, pictographs, pictures, diagrams, and maps are graphic aids.

Survey Reveals Businesses Limit Smoking	
Established policies on smoking this year	**38%**
Smoking policies under consideration	**21%**
Banned smoking in open work areas	**15%**
2%	Banned all smoking

Results of a survey of 662 employers nationwide.

DIRECTIONS Use the above graphic aid to answer the questions.

1. How many employers were surveyed? _____

2. What percentage of companies banned all smoking? _____

3. What issue is addressed in this graph? _____

DIRECTIONS Read the article and study the graph. Then complete the sentences below by circling the correct word in parentheses.

In 1980, colleges in the U.S. were turning out more teachers than the schools needed. Today, though, there is a shortage of teachers, and this shortage is projected to increase in coming years.

Where did all the teachers go? Experts say there are several explanations. When teachers outnumbered the jobs, many teachers entered other professions and have not returned. Fewer people are now preparing for the teaching profession. Women,

who used to make up a major part of the teaching force, now seek careers in fields once considered for men only.

The shortage is also due to earlier teacher retirements. Since the average age of today's teacher is forty-three, a large number will reach retirement age over the next several years. Due to retirement and mobility, it is projected that 70,000 new teachers will be needed between now and 1994.

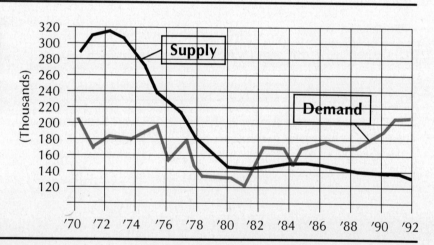

Supply and demand for teachers

(Thousands)

'70 '72 '74 '76 '78 '80 '82 '84 '86 '88 '90 '92

Source: U.S. Department of Education, National Center for Education Statistics

1. The supply of teachers in 1976 was (less / greater) than the demand.

2. The need for teachers in 1981 was the (highest / lowest) in the twenty-two year period.

3. The shortage of teachers is projected to (increase / decrease).

4. Teachers have been retiring (later / earlier) than they used to.

5. There was a sharp (rise / decline) in need from 1981 to 1982.

6. There were about the same number of teachers available as there were teaching jobs in (1978 / 1984).

7. In 1978, there about (180,000 / 220,000) teachers available.

8. The U.S. will need about 80,000 (more / fewer) teachers in 1992 than the number available.

DIRECTIONS Read the map and article. Then read each question below and circle the letter of the correct answer.

Nation

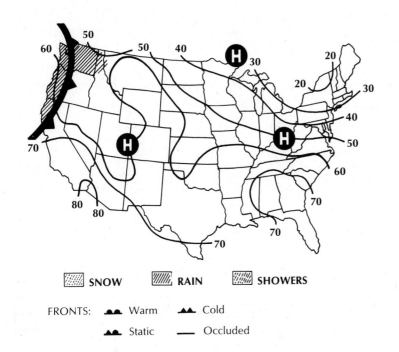

SNOW   RAIN   SHOWERS

FRONTS: Warm   Cold

Static   Occluded

A destructive storm system blamed for 21 weekend deaths tormented the Northeast Monday with snow and freezing rain, flooding creeks in western New York and forcing more than 200 residents to flee their homes.

Slick roads in northern New England caused scores of rush-hour fender benders and prompted school officials in New Hampshire to delay the start of classes.

The storm dumped 9 inches of snow in western Maine, while 7 inches fell in parts of Vermont.

Snow also fell Monday in Michigan and northern Ohio, while freezing drizzle, sleet and light snow glazed southern and central New England and the Ohio Valley.

1. In what media was the report used?
   a. book   **b.** newspaper   **c.** magazine   **d.** radio

2. Which state can expect rain?
   a. Maine   **b.** Texas   **c.** Washington   **d.** Nebraska

3. What word tells that the highest temperatures are shown?
   a. predicted   **b.** occluded   **c.** precipitation   **d.** maximum

4. What is the high temperature reported for the Southeast part of the U.S.?
   a. 70   **b.** 80   **c.** 50   **d.** 20

5. What state's school schedules were affected by weather?
   a. Michigan   **b.** Florida   **c.** New Hampshire   **d.** Ohio

6. What kind of front occurred in the Northwest?
   a. static   **b.** cold   **c.** warm   **d.** occluded

7. What condition was *not* reported in the Northeast?
   a. snow   **b.** freezing rain   **c.** sunny skies   **d.** flooding

Read the graphic aids. Then complete each statement below.

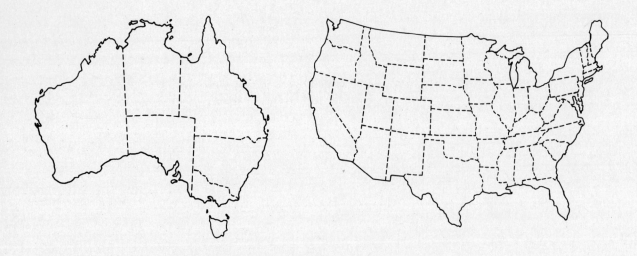

How Australia and the U.S. Compare		
	AUSTRALIA	UNITED STATES
Area:	2,967,909 sq. mi.	3,628,150 sq. mi.
Population:	15,800,000.	241,000,000.
Pop. Density:	5.2 people per sq. mi.	64 people/sq. mi.
Language:	English.	English.
Government:	Federal commonwealth. Parliamentary government headed by a prime minister, who is leader of the majority party in Parliament. Head of state is Queen Elizabeth II of the United Kingdom.	Federal republic. Two-party representative democracy, headed by an elected President. Federal government power is divided among executive, legislative, and judicial branches.
Economy:	A rich, developed nation, unusual because its wealth comes mainly from farming and mining. *Agriculture:* cattle, sheep, wheat, wool, sugarcane. *Mining:* bauxite, iron ore, lead, manganese, tin, silver, gold, uranium, copper, nickel, coal. *Manufacturing:* imports exceed exports.	Leads the world in total value of its economic production, including agriculture, mining, and manufacturing. *Agriculture:* Beef cattle, milk, corn, soybeans, hogs, wheat, cotton. *Mining:* petroleum, natural gas, coal, other minerals. *Manufacturing:* single most important U.S. economic activity.
Life Expectancy:	75 years.	75 years.

Source: *World Book Encyclopedia; 1986 World Almanac*

1. People live closer to one another in _____ than in _____ .

2. Both countries grow _____ and _____ on their farms.

3. A mining product of both countries is _____ .

4. The people of _____ do not sell as many of their own products to other countries as they buy.

Graphic aids help you understand important information.

152 Reading Graphs

Facts at a Glance

It often helps to see a group of facts rather than just read a paragraph that contains facts. In this lesson, you will learn about four kinds of graphs that let you see facts at a glance.

 KEYS to Graphs

Graphs show how facts compare to one another.

LEARN A *graph* presents information in an organized way. You can use the information to make quick comparisons, evaluate results, or note changes. A *pie* or *circle graph* shows how each part of the information is related to the whole. A key may accompany a graph to explain any symbols used.

EXAMPLE
The graph shows what part of the total profits came from each activity.

DIRECTIONS Use the facts on the above graph to answer these questions.

1. Which carnival event was the most successful money maker?

_____

2. Did Face Painting or Small Animal Zoo draw the most customers?

_____

Profit Earned at Sixth Grade Carnival

$30.00
White Elephant Sale

$25.00
Hot Dogs/Lemonade

$10.00
Talent Show

$20.00
Small Animal Zoo

$15.00
Ring Toss

$18.00
Cookie Stand

$18.00
Face Painting

3. Which carnival event produced the smallest amount of earnings?

_____

2 Practice With Graphs

DIRECTIONS   A *bar graph* shows how things compare. Each bar on the graph represents a fact. By glancing at the bars on the graph, you can see which group is the largest, the smallest, and which group or groups lie in-between. The title of a bar graph tells you what facts are being compared. Read the paragraph and menu. Study the bar graph which shows the number of students who ate hot lunches during one week. Then complete each sentence below.

The Briarton Middle School hot lunch program is a success. Students on the Middle School's student council help select the food items and publish the menu.

Hot Lunch Program

MONDAY   Hamburgers/cheese-burgers, carrots and celery, apple, cookie, milk/juice

TUESDAY   Chicken drumsticks, french fries, lima beans, orange, doughnut, milk/cider

WEDNESDAY   Spaghetti, green beans, tossed salad, fruit cup, ice cream bars, milk

THURSDAY   Hot dogs, potato chips, baked beans, grapes, brownies, milk/punch

FRIDAY   Fish sticks, mashed potato, corn, apple, pudding, milk

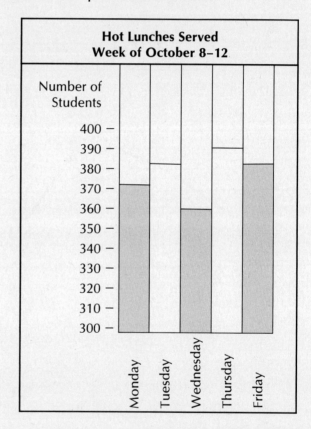

1. Three-hundred eighty-three students ate hot lunches on _____ and _____ .

2. The main course that attracted fewest students was _____ .

3. The main course that was apparently the favorite was _____ .

4. _____ students purchased hot lunches on the day baked beans were served.

5. Burgers seem to be a more appealing main dish than _____ .

6. Burgers attracted _____ students on _____ .

Read and Apply

DIRECTIONS A *line graph* shows how things change over time. Information is *plotted,* or marked by dots, on the bars of the graph. The dots are connected to show a line that goes upward as amounts increase or downward as they decrease. Two lines on a line graph show how two sets of facts compare to one another.

Read Tricia's line graph of her math and science test scores during her first quarter of the school year. Use the key to interpret the graph. Then answer each question below by circling *T* for true or *F* for false.

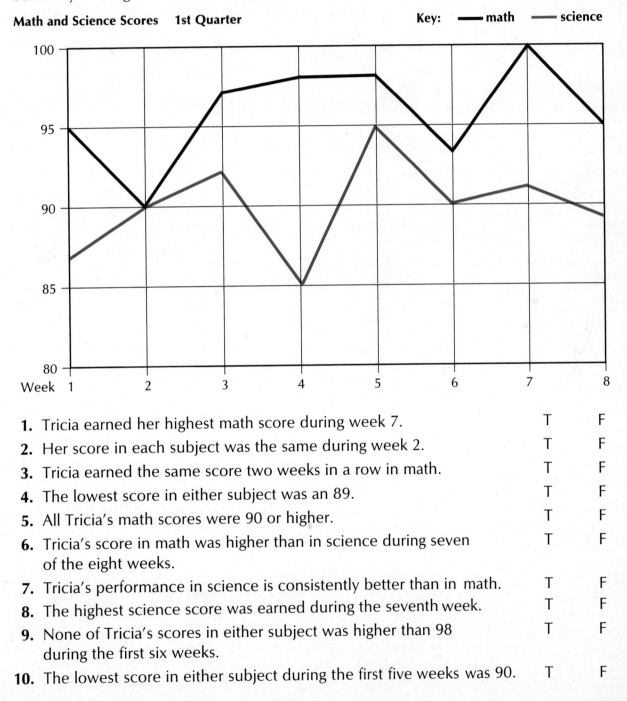

Math and Science Scores   1st Quarter   Key: ━━ math   ━━ science

1. Tricia earned her highest math score during week 7.   T   F
2. Her score in each subject was the same during week 2.   T   F
3. Tricia earned the same score two weeks in a row in math.   T   F
4. The lowest score in either subject was an 89.   T   F
5. All Tricia's math scores were 90 or higher.   T   F
6. Tricia's score in math was higher than in science during seven   T   F
   of the eight weeks.
7. Tricia's performance in science is consistently better than in math. T   F
8. The highest science score was earned during the seventh week.   T   F
9. None of Tricia's scores in either subject was higher than 98   T   F
   during the first six weeks.
10. The lowest score in either subject during the first five weeks was 90. T   F

A *picture graph* uses pictures instead of bars to compare things. The pictures tell you what the graph is comparing. Each picture stands for a number. The *legend* tells what each picture represents. Read the paragraph. Then read the picture graph and legend and answer the questions below.

Mrs. Lynch taught her class to read picture graphs. Each student gathered facts from three friends. Then the students summarized and recorded their facts on picture graphs.

Total Hours of Television Viewing: Rob, Angel, Debbie Sunday, April 18 to Saturday, April 24
April 18: 📺📺📺📺📺📺📺📺📺🬀
April 19: 📺📺📺📺📺
April 20: 📺📺📺📺📺📺📺📺📺📺
April 21: 📺📺📺
April 22: 📺📺📺📺📺📺🬀
April 23: 📺📺📺📺🬀
April 24: 📺📺📺📺📺📺📺📺📺📺📺🬀

Legend

📺 = 1 hour

🬀 = 45 minutes

🬀 = 30 minutes

1. On which days did Rob, Angel, and Debbie watch at least ten hours of television?

_____

_____

2. Did the students watch television more on Monday or Friday?

_____

How much more? _____

3. If each student watched an equal number of hours on April 19, how many hours did each child watch?

_____

4. How much more TV was watched on April 24 than on April 20?

_____

5. Did the students watch more TV during the week or on the week-end?

_____

6. How many hours of television did the students watch on April 21?

_____

REMEMBER Graphs allow you to compare facts at a glance.

An Organized View

Information is often presented in chart form to give an organized overview. In this lesson, you'll learn about charts and their uses.

KEYS to Charts

A chart is a graphic display of organized information.

LEARN   A *chart* shows information in an organized way. Data on a chart may be in numbers, words, or symbols. To find a fact, read down a column and across a row.

EXAMPLE   STUDENT TRANSPORTATION
Edgewood Middle School

	Grade 6	Grade 7	Grade 8
Walk	82	94	78
Bus #2	27	16	7
Bus #14	17	3	30
Bus #26	12	31	8

To find the number of walkers in grade 7, read across the chart from *walk* to the *grade 7 column*. There are 94 walkers in grade 7.

DIRECTIONS Use the above chart to complete the sentences.

1. The chart gives information about the _____ of students to Edgewood Middle School.

2. The bus with the most seventh graders is Bus _____ .

3. The smallest number of walkers is in grade _____ .

4. Bus 2 has more students from grade _____ than any other grade.

2 Practice With Charts

DIRECTIONS Businesses and industries often use charts to summarize income during a year or over an extended period of time. A summary chart allows the administrators to see how well each part of their business is doing. A chart is often preferred to a written report, since the figures can be studied at a glance. Read the paragraph and chart. Then complete the work below.

Matthew's business, Ryan Enterprises, is thriving. Matthew prepared the following chart to depict his earnings:

INCOME STATEMENT

Ryan Enterprises, Inc. 1985–1987			
Service	1985	1986	1987
Babysitting	$520	$680	$710
Lawn Mowing	96	108	120
Pet Sitting	50	46	55
Snow Shoveling	70	110	90
Gardening	–0–	38	29
Golf Caddying	80	75	–0–
Corn Detassling	–0–	–0–	300
Total Earnings	$816	$1,057	$1,304

1. During what year did Matthew begin Ryan Enterprises, Inc.?

2. How many years has Matthew earned money by offering each of the following services?

   Babysitting _____

   Gardening _____

   Pet Sitting _____

   Corn Detassling _____

3. Which services showed an increased income in 1986 and again in 1987?

4. Did Matthew's total income increase from 1985 to 1986?

   from 1986 to 1987?

5. Which service continued to provide Matthew's best source of income year after year?

6. How much income did the Golf Caddying service earn for the business in 1987?

7. Which service provided

   a. eighty dollars in 1985?

   b. no income in 1987?

   c. just under one hundred dollars in 1987?

3   Read and Apply

DIRECTIONS   Many businesses and industries use a *flow chart* to show the structure of a company's management. A flow chart may show a plan for how a task is to be completed. Read the paragraph and circle the letter of the best answer below.

When Ms. Foote became president of Optic Industries, her goal was to expand production and sales over the next five years. As part of her long-range planning, Ms. Foote proposed some staff additions and some changes in the roles performed by present employees. She worked from the company's current flow chart to create a proposed chart that showed her recommended changes.

CURRENT STRUCTURE

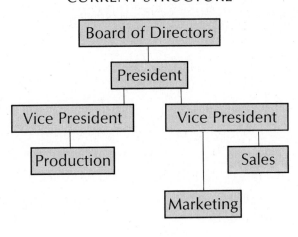

PROPOSED STRUCTURE

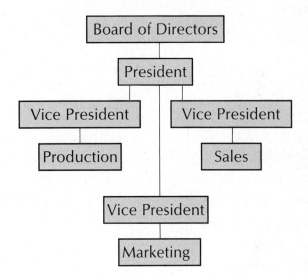

1. The company's current management structure shows
   a. Two vice-presidents.
   b. A vice-president in charge of production.
   c. A vice-president in charge of sales and marketing.
   d. All of the above.

2. The proposed structure for the company's management
   a. Would require one less vice-president.
   b. Would require an additional vice-president.
   c. Would place one vice-president in charge of sales and production.
   d. Would place a vice-president in charge of marketing and sales.

Charts can be convenient reference sources. Read the chart which gives plant-diet information for roses. Then complete each sentence below by circling the letter of the correct answer.

ELEMENT	CONTRIBUTION	SIGNS OF POOR NUTRITION
Nitrogen	Promotes green growth (too much produces leaves but no flowers)	Leaves turn yellow. Flowers are small and pale. Buds don't open. Little new growth occurs.
Potassium	Much growth	Stems are weak. Buds don't fully form. Leaves turn brown.
Calcium	Good, strong roots	Roots are deformed and weak.
Sulfur	Good, green growth	New leaves turn yellow.
Chlorine	Good, green growth	Leaves form poorly.
Copper	Good, green growth	Tips of plants don't form fully.
Iron	Assures green plants	Leaves are yellow.
Phosphorus	Promotes good flowers and strong roots	Leaves fall too early. Stems are weak. Buds are slow in opening. Leaves are dull green. Roots are abnormal.

1. A rose plant that produces buds that never open may need
   a. potassium.
   b. nitrogen.
   c. chlorine.
   d. all of the above.

2. When rose bushes have strong roots and produce lovely roses, they have
   a. adequate phosphorus.
   b. too much nitrogen.
   c. not had enough iron.
   d. not received enough phosphorus.

3. Rosebuds that are slow in opening
   a. are the result of too little chlorine.
   b. cause leaves to be dull green.
   c. are the result of too little phosphorus.
   d. cause good root development.

4. Some signs of insufficient potassium are
   a. when rose leaves turn brown.
   b. when rose stems are weak.
   c. when buds are not fully formed.
   d. all of the above.

REMEMBER A chart gives organized facts at a glance.

Let It Snow, Let It Snow, Let It Snow!

Which state in the U.S. has the heaviest snowfall? In this lesson, you'll read about snowfall as you learn to use some graphic aids.

 ## 1 KEYS to Charts and Graphs

Charts and graphs show data at a glance.

LEARN *Charts* and *graphs* are graphic presentations of information. Both present data in an organized way for quick reference and interpretation.

EXAMPLE

Record Snowfalls in United States				
Date	Location	Inches	Centimeters	Period
1911	Tamarack, California	390	991	1 month
1921	Silver Lake, Colorado	76	193	24 hours
1971–1972	Rainier Paradise Ranger Station, Washington	1,122	2,850	1 season

DIRECTIONS Use the above chart to complete each sentence.

1. A record snowfall of _____ inches fell in one day in Colorado in 1921.

2. _____ centimeters of snow blanketed an area in the state of Washington during a one-year period.

3. In 1911, a record snowfall of three-hundred-ninety inches was recorded in

   _____ .

4. An area in Colorado holds the record for the most snow in any _____ period.

Charts and Graphs **161**

2 Practice With Charts and Graphs

DIRECTIONS Study the bar graph. Then answer the questions below.

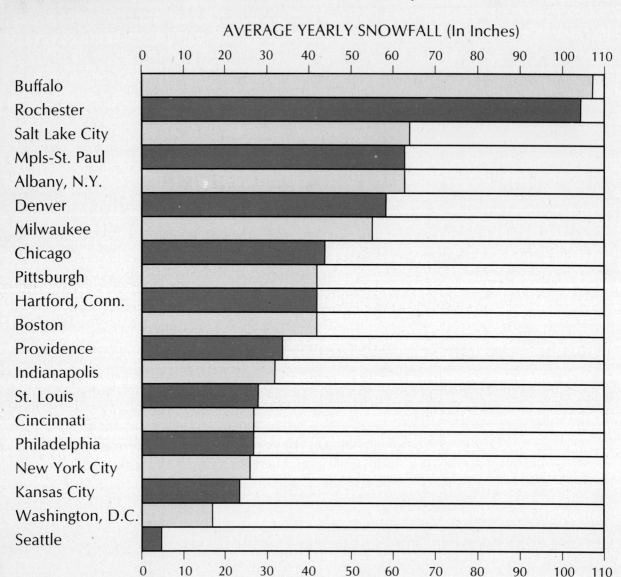

AVERAGE YEARLY SNOWFALL (In Inches)

1. Approximately how many inches of snow does Rochester get each year?

_____

2. Would you expect to experience more or less snow in your new community if you moved from Indianapolis, Indiana to Albany, New York?

_____

3. Which is the snowier city, Chicago or Providence?

_____

4. What two cities have the same average yearly snowfall as Hartford, Connecticut?

_____

_____

Charts and Graphs **162**

3 Read and Apply

DIRECTIONS Read about snowfalls.

Residents of Los Angeles, Houston, Atlanta, and Miami aren't too concerned about snowfall since those cities rarely, if ever, are affected. Those who live in Seattle, Louisville, and Baltimore only encounter snow occasionally, but the lives of people in Minneapolis, Buffalo, and Rochester are greatly affected by snow.

There are two ways to identify how much snow an area has. The first is by the total snowfall during the year. Syracuse, New York, for example, gets about 112 inches of snow a year. When snow falls in Syracuse, and most other places in the North, it stays until spring when the weather warms up.

Another way to measure the snowiness of an area is to examine the snow cover on the ground. Snow cover is the number of inches of snow that accumulates on the ground. Little Rock, Arkansas, for example, will get snow occasionally, but it generally melts after a few hours. In some parts of the country, the ground may be covered with two or three inches of snow for a month or two. In other parts of the country, the ground may be covered with over twenty inches of snow for up to three months.

The state of New York is the home of the nation's snowiest cities. Buffalo accumulates more snow than any other large city in the country. Storms collect moisture as they sweep across Lake Erie to dump the white fluff on Buffalo. As snowstorms continue east, they hit Rochester, N.Y. making it the second snowiest big city in the U.S.

Although Buffalo and Rochester top the list of large metropolitan areas, the smaller cities of Syracuse and Watertown, N.Y. actually receive more snow.

City	Snowfall*
Buffalo, New York	1,067.3
Rochester, New York	1,037.7
Salt Lake City, Utah	638.8
Minneapolis-St. Paul, Minnesota	632.1
Albany, New York	631.6
Cleveland, Ohio	627.0
Denver, Colorado	584.0
Milwaukee, Wisconsin	551.3
Detroit, Michigan	463.3
Chicago, Illinois	438.9
Pittsburgh, Pennsylvania	421.1
Hartford, Connecticut	418.1
Boston, Massachusetts	416.8
Providence, Rhode Island	343.6
Dayton, Ohio	334.6
Indianapolis, Indiana	324.5
Columbus, Ohio	316.9
St. Louis, Missouri	275.7
Cincinnati, Ohio	269.9
Philadelphia, Pennsylvania	267.0

*(in inches)

1. Rank the cities in Ohio in order from most to least snowfall.

   a. _____

   b. _____

   c. _____

   d. _____

2. Which states have two or more large cities with abundant snowfalls?

   a. Wisconsin, Pennsylvania, and Ohio

   b. New York, Missouri, and Pennsylvania

   c. New York, Ohio, and Pennsylvania

   d. None of the above

3. Which state's twin cities had 632.1 inches of snow in the ten-year period?

   a. Minnesota

   b. Pennsylvania

   c. Missouri

   d. Ohio

REMEMBER Graphs and charts make quick reference easy.

World Religions

Why does *B.C.* or *A.D.* often precede or follow a date? In this lesson, you'll learn about the difference between *B.C* and *A.D.* as you learn to read timelines. You'll also read about religions of the world.

 ## 1 KEYS to Timelines

A timeline shows events in order.

LEARN   A *timeline* is a horizontal line with dates marked in order across it. An event is noted at each date. A timeline gives a quick picture of the relationship of events that happen over a period of time.

| 800 B.C. | 700 B.C. | 600 B.C. | 500 B.C. | 400 B.C. | 300 B.C. | 200 B.C. | 100 B.C. | Birth of Christ | A.D. 100 | A.D. 200 | A.D. 300 | A.D. 400 | A.D. 500 | A.D. 600 | A.D. 700 | A.D. 800 |

Most of the Western world uses the Gregorian calendar, which numbers years to show the time before and after the birth of Jesus Christ. Years marked *B.C.* came before the birth of Jesus Christ. Years marked *A.D.* (Latin for *in the year of our Lord*) are after the birth of Christ.

DIRECTIONS   Use the timeline above to complete the work.

1. Draw a wavy mark on the timeline to show the section of time from 500 B.C. to 50 B.C.

2. The Temple of Diana is one of the ancient wonders of the world. It was built in A.D. 262. Mark an *X* on the timeline to show *about* when the temple was built.

2 Practice With Timelines

DIRECTIONS This timeline of medical milestones shows the time relationships between important medical events. Use the timeline as you read each sentence below and circle the correct word or words in parentheses.

Chinese use acupuncture — 2700 B.C.

First laws written on diet/cleanliness — 600 B.C.

Hippocrates wrote oath for doctors — 400 B.C.

Before Christ   **Anno Domini**

microscope invented — A.D. 1590

stethoscope invented — A.D. 1819

1st X-rays — A.D. 1895

1st microsurgery — A.D. 1921

penicillin found — A.D. 1928

polio vaccine discovered — A.D. 1954

1. The earliest medical fact recorded on this timeline is (acupuncture / microsurgery).

2. Penicillin (had / had not) been discovered by the time the doctors first performed microsurgery.

3. Hippocrates wrote the medical "oath of ethics" (before / after) the birth of Jesus Christ.

4. The first microsurgeons were able to use (penicillin / the X-ray) .

5. Doctors were unable to use penicillin to treat patients in (1934 / 1926) .

DIRECTIONS Add each fact in its correct place on the above timeline.

a. 1864 A.D.—pasteurization discovered
b. 1628 A.D.—discovery that blood circulates
c. 1500 B.C.—papyrus scrolls on surgery written

Read and Apply

DIRECTIONS Read about major religions of the world.

Buddhism, Christianity, Confucianism, Hinduism, Islam, Judaism, and Taoism are major world religions. Each has its own way of teaching people to live, and each has a place of importance in world history.

The Buddhist religion was founded around 500 B.C. by Prince Siddhartha Guatama, the Buddha. Buddhists worship Buddha and read about his teachings in a sacred book, the *Tripitaka*. They practice yoga and meditation. They believe in reincarnation, or that people are reborn over and over. The goal of a Buddhist is to reach Nirvana, an enlightened stage in the life cycle.

Followers of Jesus Christ founded Christianity about 4 A.D. Christianity has the most followers of all the world's religions. The *New Testament* is the story of Christ's life and teachings as well as a book of historical information. Many different groups of Christians, or denominations, follow Christ's teachings. Each denomination interprets the *Bible* in a slightly different way. Christians believe Christ died on the cross and was raised from the dead. They believe that after death they will be united with God.

Confucianism is mainly practiced in China, Japan, and Mongolia. Followers of Confucius worship their ancestors and many gods. They believe they will spend their afterlife with their ancestors. Sacred books of the Confucists are the *Analects* and the *Wu Ching*. The religion, founded in China around 600 B.C. by Confucius, has no ministers.

India is the home of most followers of Hinduism. No one can become, or be converted to, Hinduism, since people are born into the religion. No one knows who founded Hinduism, but it has been practiced since 1500 B.C. The *Veda*, a book of rituals, myths, and epic stories, guides Hindus in their religious lives. Like Buddhists, Hindus believe in a cycle of birth and rebirth. During their lives on earth, Hindus serve hundreds of gods and goddesses.

The Prophet Mohammed established the Islam religion in 622 A.D. in Arabia. Moslems, as followers of Islam are called, read a holy book called the *Koran*. The *Koran* is a record of messages Allah, or God, gave to Mohammed. Moslems believe that after death their souls live on.

The *Torah* is the book that instructs the Jewish people about how to live an ethical life. Jews were the first to believe that one God created the entire universe and rules over it. Judaism, founded by Abraham over 5,000 years ago, is today mainly practiced in Israel, the United States, and the U.S.S.R.

Taoism was founded in China around 100 B.C. It is related to early Chinese folk religions. Taoists strive to be close to nature. They try to achieve harmony with nature through meditation and special diets. Taoist priests, who perform the religious rituals, must be born into a family of priests.

DIRECTIONS Use the article to create a timeline showing when each of the seven religions was founded. Then use your timeline to answer the questions.

| 4000 B.C. | 3000 B.C. | 2000 B.C. | 1000 B.C. | 1000 A.D. |

1. What is the newest of the world's religions?

   _____

2. What two religions were founded at about the same time?

   _____

   _____

3. According to the information shown on this timeline, were more religions founded *before* or *after* the birth of Jesus Christ?

   _____

4. Were the teachings of Buddha followed in 1800 B.C.?

   _____

5. What is the oldest religious group shown on this timeline?

   _____

6. Could Lao-Tze, founder of Taoism, have read Islam's Koran?

   _____

REMEMBER A timeline shows time relationships.

Finding Books at the Library

When you go to the library, do you know how to locate a book by your favorite author, or a book about a subject or person you're interested in? In this lesson, you will learn about finding books at the library.

1 KEYS to Finding Books

To find a book, know whether it is fiction, biography, or nonfiction.

LEARN   Fiction books are arranged alphabetically by authors' last names. Biographies are arranged by the last names of the persons about whom they are written. Nonfiction books are arranged according to the Dewey Decimal Classification System.

Fiction books are about imaginary events and characters. If there are several books by different authors with the same last name, the first names are used. For example, a book by <u>Jeff</u> Brown would be shelved before a book by <u>Marcia</u> Brown.

When one author has written several fiction books, the titles are used to arrange the books alphabetically. The articles <u>a</u>, <u>an</u>, and <u>the</u>, when they are the first word, are not used. These books by Constance C. Green would be shelved in this order: *Alexander the Great, Ask Anybody, A Girl Called Al.*

DIRECTIONS   Number these books in the John D. Fitzgerald *Great Brain* series from 1 to 7 to show the correct order for shelving. The first two have been done for you.

_____ The Return of the Great Brain   _____ The Great Brain Does It Again

__1__ The Great Brain   _____ Me and My Little Brain

__2__ The Great Brain at the Academy   _____ The Great Brain Reforms

_____ More Adventures of the Great Brain

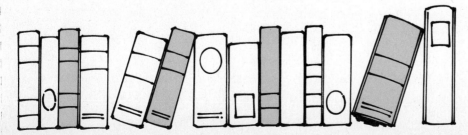

2   Practice Finding Books

DIRECTIONS   Here is a list of fiction books. Put the books in the correct order for shelving by numbering them 1 through 10. Two have been numbered.

_____ *No Ponies for Miss Pobjoy* by Ursula Moray Williams

_____ *The Cat Who Wished to be a Man* by Lloyd Alexander

___3___ *The Blossoms Meet the Vulture Lady* by Betsy Byars

_____ *Henry Reed's Think Tank* by Keith Robertson

_____ *The Pet-Sitting Peril* by Willo Davis Roberts.

_____ *A Crown for a Queen* by Ursula Moray Williams

_____ *Connie* by Anne Alexander

___6___ *Dannie Dunn and the Automatic House* by Jay Williams

_____ *The Toymaker's Daughter* by Ursula Moray Williams

_____ *Winter Wheat* by Jeanne Williams

DIRECTIONS   Nonfiction books about real people are called biographies. If a person writes a book about himself or herself, it is called an autobiography. These books are usually shelved in a special section of the library. Like fiction books, they are arranged alphabetically, but they are alphabetized according to the last name of the person written about, rather than by the author's last name.

Arrange these biographies in the proper order from 1 to 5.

_____ *Abe Lincoln Grows Up* by Carl Sandburg

_____ *The Story of Florence Nightingale* by Margaret Leighton

_____ *Daniel Boone* by James Daugherty

_____ *Winged Moccasins, the Story of Sacajawea* by Frances Joyce Farnsworth

_____ *Amos Fortune, Free Man* by Elizabeth Yates

3 Read and Apply

DIRECTIONS Nonfiction books other than biographies are often arranged on library shelves according to the Dewey Decimal Classification System. This system organizes books into ten major categories. Books in each category have special numbers assigned to them. The first three numbers indicate the main category. These three numbers are followed by a decimal point and more numbers, which further subdivide the category. Here are the ten major categories of the Dewey Decimal Classification System.

NUMBERS	MAJOR CATEGORY	SOME SUBJECTS IN THE CATEGORY
000–099	General Works	Computers, journalism, reference works
100–199	Philosophy and Psychology	Human knowledge, behavior, and feelings
200–299	Religion	Religions, mythology
300–399	Social Sciences	Women, families, Black history, law, economics, education, holidays
400–499	Language	Dictionaries, study of languages
500–599	Science	Mathematics, astronomy, physics, chemistry, geology, biology, science experiments
600–699	Applied Science or Useful Arts	Inventions, medicine and health, engineering, farming, gardening, cooking, sewing, pets
700–799	Arts and Recreation	Painting, sculpture, drawing, photography, music, crafts, sports, games, radio, television
800–899	Literature	Poetry, plays, essays
900–999	Geography, History and Travel	Ancient and modern history, geography, travel

Read the titles of these nonfiction books and decide what main category and Dewey Decimal number range the librarian would use to shelve the books. The first one has been done for you.

BOOK TITLE	MAIN CATEGORY	NUMBER RANGE
Drawing Cartoon Characters	Arts and Recreation	700–799
Poems Here and Now		
Know Your Feelings		
Fun With Spanish		
Understanding Africa		
Kids and Computers		
World Religions		
The Amish Family		
The Universe		
Giants of Invention		

DIRECTIONS Here is a list of five book titles. Write an F on the line if the book is fiction, a B if it is biography, and an NF if it is nonfiction.

1. _____ The Usborne Book of Puzzles

2. _____ The Dollhouse Murders

3. _____ Confessions of an Orange Octopus

4. _____ The Story of George Washington Carver

5. _____ Lights Out! Kids Talk About Summer Camp

REMEMBER Fiction books, biographies, and nonfiction books are shelved in different ways in libraries.

Using the Card Catalog

When you go to the library, you may know the title of a fiction book you want, but not the author. On the other hand, you may like a particular author, or want to find books on a specific subject. The library's card catalog can help you. In this lesson, you will learn about the card catalog and how it can help you get specific information about books.

 ## KEYS to Using the Card Catalog

Every book in the library has a title, author, and subject card.

LEARN The card catalog does not look like a catalog. It is a cabinet of drawers filled with cards filed in alphabetical order. The drawers are labeled to show what letters are inside. A card catalog looks like this:

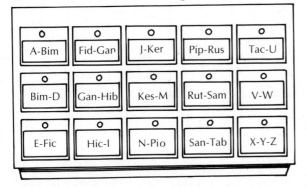

To find books on the subject of whales, look in the drawer labeled <u>V-W</u>. To find the title of a book by an author whose last name is <u>Glanzer</u>, look in the drawer labeled <u>Gan-Hib</u>. To find the author of a book called *The Talking Earth,* look in the drawer labeled <u>Tac-U</u>. (Remember, the articles <u>a</u>, <u>an</u>, and <u>the</u> are not used for alphabetizing titles.)

DIRECTIONS Write down the letters of the drawers you would open to look for the following cards:

1. Books by Marcia Brown _____

2. Books on the subject of football _____

3. Books on the subject of television _____

4. A book titled *The Stonewalkers* _____

2 # Practice Using the Card Catalog

DIRECTIONS In the card catalog, there are three kinds of cards for each book: an *author* card, a *title* card, and a *subject* card. The same information is printed on each card. The author card, however, has the author's name at the top and is filed under the author's last name. The title card has the title at the top and is filed under the first word of the title (except when it is *a, an,* or *the*). The subject card has the subject of the book printed at the top of the card and is filed under the first word of the subject.

Here are samples of the top sections of three cards, all for the same nonfiction book. Because it is nonfiction, the call number is written on each card.

796.81   ARNEIL, STEVE
              DOWLER, BRYAN

              Modern Karate

Chicago: Henry Regnery, 1974

AUTHOR CARD (authors listed first)

796.81   MODERN KARATE

              Arneil, Steve
              Dowler, Bryan

Chicago: Henry Regnery, 1974

TITLE CARD (title listed first)

796.81   MARTIAL ARTS

              Arneil, Steve
              Dowler, Bryan

              Modern Karate

Chicago: Henry Regnery, 1974

SUBJECT CARD (subject listed first)

Answer the questions about the sample cards shown above.

1. What is the title of the book? _____

2. Who are the authors of the book? _____

3. What is the subject of the book? _____

4. In which drawer of the card catalog on page 173 would you find the author card?

_____

5. In which drawer would you find the subject card? _____

6. In which drawer would you find the title card? _____

3 | Read and Apply

DIRECTIONS Study this complete sample card from the card catalog.

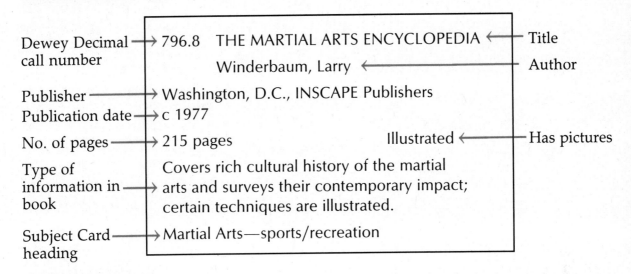

Dewey Decimal call number → 796.8   THE MARTIAL ARTS ENCYCLOPEDIA ← Title

Winderbaum, Larry ← Author

Publisher → Washington, D.C., INSCAPE Publishers
Publication date → c 1977

No. of pages → 215 pages   Illustrated ← Has pictures

Type of information in book → Covers rich cultural history of the martial arts and surveys their contemporary impact; certain techniques are illustrated.

Subject Card heading → Martial Arts—sports/recreation

DIRECTIONS Answer the questions about the library book for the sample card. Use the information that is printed on the card.

1. Is this book fiction or nonfiction?

_____

2. How can you tell?

_____

_____

3. Is the sample card a subject card, title card, or author card?

_____

4. How can you tell?

_____

_____

5. Who is the author of the book?

_____

6. What is the title of the book?

_____

_____

7. Where was the book published?

_____

When? _____

8. Who is the publishing company?

_____

9. How many pages are in the book?

_____

10. Is it illustrated? _____

Read each situation below. Write the key words you would use to find cards in the card catalog for the books you would need. Then tell whether you would be looking for a subject card, author card, or title card. The first one has been done for you.

1. You need to write a report on the heart for science.

   Key Words ___heart_____ Type of Card ___subject___

2. You want to start a new hobby, but you don't know exactly what to choose.

   Key Words _____ Type of Card _____

3. Your friend has convinced you to read some of Todd Strasser's books.

   Key Words _____ Type of Card _____

4. The literature teacher has assigned the book *Cheaper by the Dozen*. You want to check it out of the library.

   Key Words _____ Type of Card _____

5. You have read the book *Tae Kwon Do* and want to learn more about the martial arts.

   Key Words _____ Type of Card _____

6. You have just read C. S. Lewis' *Chronicles of Narnia* and want to find out what other books the author has written.

   Key Words _____ Type of Card _____

7. You have just read a review of *Interstellar Pig* in a magazine. You can't wait to find the book and begin reading it!

   Key Words _____ Type of Card _____

8. You heard some friends talking about sign language. You want to find a book that would teach some of the signs.

   Key Words _____ Type of Card _____

REMEMBER   Every book in the library is in the card catalog.

Trivia and More

What were the highest and lowest temperatures recorded in your area last year? How many women are in the United States Marines? What is the population of the world's largest city? In this lesson, you will learn about a reference book that holds these answers and more.

1 KEYS to Using an Almanac

An almanac is a book of useful facts.

LEARN An *almanac* contains interesting and useful information. Most almanacs are published every year with up-to-date facts. Special almanacs focus on topics like sports or farming, while general almanacs span a wide range of subject areas. Most almanacs have a brief index for quick reference in addition to a general index. As in all reference books, facts may be found under several different subject headings.

EXAMPLE Facts about a person in history may be found under the person's name, country, contribution, and perhaps other subject headings. Population figures might be found under *World Population, Census,* individual country names, *World Facts,* etc.

DIRECTIONS Write two or more subject areas under which you might look in an index for information on each topic. The first one is done for you.

1. Time ___clocks, calendars, sun, time zones___

2. Taxes _____

3. Space _____

4. Courts _____

5. Medicine _____

6. Soccer _____

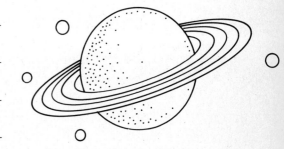

Practice Using an Almanac

DIRECTIONS Use the partial *table of contents* from an almanac to write the page numbers you'd check to find each answer below.

CABINET, U.S. 314–318, 321–324, 705
CALENDARS 360–362, 717–755
CANADA 695–715
CITIES OF NORTH
    AMERICA 113, 251–253, 660–669
COLLEGES AND UNIVERSITIES 215–242
COMPUTERS 114, 116

CONGRESSIONAL ACTIONS 924–925
CONGRESSIONAL ELECTIONS 72–80
CONSUMER AND INFORMATION
    OFFICES 107–108
COPYRIGHT LAW 685–686
CRIME 789–794

1. How many students attended Ohio State University in 1986?

2. What is Canada's national symbol?

DIRECTIONS An *index* is more specific than a table of contents. Use the partial index to write the page numbers on which you would find information about each subject below.

Ford, Gerald R. 309–318
    Assassination attempts (1975) 693–694
    Nixon's pardon (1974) 484
    Vice President (1973) 483
Ford, Henry 386
    Motor Co. 196, 478
Forefathers' Day 754
Forest land by state 183
    (see individual states)
Forms of address 454–455
Formulas, mathematical 771
Ft. Ticonderoga (1776, 1777) 474
Fort Worth, Tex. 662
    Buildings, tall 672–673
    City manager 85
    Police roster 794

                    –G–

Galileo (1633) 498, 499
Gambia 540
    Aid, U.S. 602
    Ambassadors 603
Gardens—
    Charleston, S.C. 651

    Longwood, Pa. 650
    Peace, N. Dak. 648
Gasoline—
    Automobile consumption 123
    Average retail price 177
    Cost 177
    Energy value 124
Guam 657
    Altitudes (high, low) 433
    Cities (population) 302
    Congressional delegate 80
    Governor 83
    Population 302
Guatemala 494, 544, 909
    Aid, U.S. 602
    Ambassadors 603
    Earthquake (1976) 688
    Emigration to U.S. 254
    Government 544
    Volcanoes 622
Gulf Coast, length 433
Gymnastics 840

1. Population of Guam _____

2. Gymnastics meets _____

3. Police in Fort Worth, Texas _____

4. President Nixon's pardon by Gerald

Ford _____

5. Gardens of Longwood, Pa. _____

6. Volcanoes in Guatemala _____

7. Forefather's day _____

8. Mathematical formulas _____

3 Read and Apply

DIRECTIONS Read about how an almanac may be an idea resource.

Suppose you have a report to do and the subject is entirely open. That leaves you with thousands of possible subjects, doesn't it? Or suppose a general subject is given, and you need to choose a specific topic. Where would you begin?

Turn to an almanac. If you've been given a general subject, think of all the possible words under which you might find information on the subject in an almanac's index. Look up each reference and read about the subject. One of those bits of information just might capture your interest and help you decide on a topic for your report.

If you're given no topic, an almanac can be your idea reference book. First, you may want to find an almanac that contains a *Quick Reference Index*. Scan this index to see if any of the general topics piques your interest. If so, refer to the pages listed and begin to read for

facts that can help focus your attention on a specific aspect of the topic.

If you're not intrigued by any of the general subject areas, turn to the almanac's general index and leaf through the pages as you scan for topic ideas.

Still at a loss for a topic? Don't despair! Clear your mind for a few moments and just flip through the almanac. Quickly scan the bold-faced words on the pages. When a subject interests you, stop and read the passage. Move on whenever you like and read another section. Continue doing this for a while and then ask yourself if any of what you've read might be material for an interesting report.

You just might be surprised to find you're beginning to "nail it down." In any case, you will have learned some interesting trivia in the process.

Use the page from an almanac's index to write the page numbers on which you would find the information given in each statement below.

United States of America
Agencies, government 317
Constitution 443–450
Flag 455–456
Military training centers 329–330
Monuments, national 438–439
Passports 103
Public schools 212
Uruguay 627–628
Aid, U.S. 637
Ambassadors 639
Utah 665
Name, Origin 435
Population
—Black and Hispanic 225
—Cities and towns 255
—Counties, county seats 272
—Density 220
U-2 flights 481

–V–

Vancouver, Br. Col., Can. 681
Buildings, tall 689
Population 681
Vesuvius, Mt. (Italy) (79 A.D.) 534
Veterans Administration 116, 328
Vice presidents of the U.S. 307–309
Nominees .307, 485
Salary 317
Succession to presidency 450
Victoria Day 744
Video cassette recorders 97
Vietnam War 511, 512, 629–630
Agent Orange suit (1984) 485
Medal of Honor .335
Peace pacts (1973) 483

1. The population of Brigham City, Utah, a county seat, is 5,614 people.

_____

2. Persons over 13 years of age must appear in person to apply for a U.S. passport.

_____

3. There are nearly forty million students enrolled in public elementary and secondary schools in the United States.

_____

4. Mt. Vesuvius, a volcano overlooking Naples Bay, erupted in 79 A.D. and engulfed Pompeii.

_____

5. The vice president of the U.S. earns $91,000 per year plus $10,000 for expenses.

_____

6. The origin of Utah's name is a Navajo word which means _upper_ or _higher up._

_____

7. The world famous sculpture of four presidents is at Mount Rushmore, an area of 1,278 acres set aside in South Dakota in 1925 as a national monument.

_____

8. A total of 239 Medal of Honor awards have been awarded to date for bravery in Vietnam.

_____

9. Malkom R. Wilkey is the current U.S. Ambassador to Uruguay.

_____

10. Fort Dix, New Jersey and Fort Knox, Kentucky are two of some twenty-five principal U.S. Military Training Centers.

_____

REMEMBER An almanac has the answers!

No Loss for Words

Do the words *good, nice,* and *awesome* describe something in exactly the same way? In this lesson, you'll learn about a book that gives a wide choice of synonyms so you will never be at a loss for words.

1 KEYS to the Thesaurus

A thesaurus is a guide to words with the same or similar meaning.

LEARN   A *thesaurus* is a book of synonyms. Like a dictionary, a thesaurus has *guide words* and *entry words*. Guide words at the top of a page help you find entry words which are listed in alphabetical order. Entry words are not defined, since a thesaurus is not a dictionary. An entry word is followed by a list of synonyms to help you find the exact word to express a thought. Some thesauruses also list antonyms for entry words.

EXAMPLE   *inactive:* idle, inert, latent, quiescent, passive, motionless, stagnant, sedentary, resting, dormant, lazy, inanimate, torpid, indolent. *Ant.* active, working, acting, moving, bustling, energetic, live, dynamic.

DIRECTIONS Read the precise meaning of each synonym for *inactive*. Then answer the question below.

    A. sedentary—sitting most of the time.
    B. passive—not acting involved
    C. dormant—resting and temporarily inactive

1. Which word might describe a quiet audience that fails to applaud?

_____

Practice With the Thesaurus

DIRECTIONS All three patients are unwell. However, each of the terms used to discuss their sicknesses gives a slightly different feeling about how sick each patient really is. Most people would agree that Conrad is in the most serious shape with his *disease.* John is a little better off with his *illness,* and Martha is almost well, or just *ailing.* No two synonyms mean exactly the same thing. Words differ in intensity, size, or the amount of feeling they convey.

Choose the best synonym from each group of words to complete each sentence.

1. fragile   dainty   delicate

   a. The pages in this old book are very _____ .

   b. The tiny newborn baby's fingers are _____ .

   c. There are hundreds of _____ stitches in this needlework piece.

2. cry   whine   sob

   a. Feeling disappointed, Meredith began to _____ softly.

   b. The newborn puppies will probably _____ all night.

   c. The actress must _____ hysterically in this scene.

3. demand   ask   request

   a. After six months, Steve made a formal _____ for a raise.

   b. Marty will _____ six friends to come to the party.

   c. The baby cried angrily to _____ its bottle.

182 Using a Thesaurus

Read and Apply

DIRECTIONS Use the sample entries from a thesaurus to replace the underlined word in each paragraph below. Write the synonym on the line.

house: abode, residence, dwelling, habitation, cottage, shanty, shack, hut

howl: bellow, shriek, wail, yowl

huge: tremendous, gigantic, vast; *ant.* tiny, miniature, small, diminutive

hurt: damage, pain, injury, wound; *ant.* heal, cure, remedy, please

husky: strong, sturdy, powerful, robust, healthy, hoarse, throaty

1. The <u>house</u> on the lake looked as if it had been deserted for years. At one time it had probably been a summer home for a family. Carefully, Willy opened the sagging door and dragged himself inside the dank, dingy shelter.

   _____

2. Darkness was rapidly approaching. Willy could barely see across the deserted lake. He shivered as a loud, piercing <u>howl</u> shattered the dark, shadowy woodlot to his left.

   _____

3. Fearfully, peering out of what was once a window, Willy saw the outline of a <u>huge</u> animal. Would the animal dare venture any closer to the building? Willy shivered once again.

   _____

4. The <u>hurt</u> in his leg made him feel weak but Willy knew he must do something quickly. He must not give the animal time to overcome his fear of humans and approach the shelter.

   _____

5. Gathering all the strength he had, Willy yelled out a <u>husky</u>, "Shoo, get away from here!" To his relief, the animal turned and trotted back into the woodlot.

   _____

A thesaurus entry often includes a reference to another word or words where more synonyms can be found. The word *see* is followed by specific words. An entry word's part of speech is often given, and synonyms that are considered slang words are sometimes included. Use the thesaurus entries to complete each sentence.

correct, v. & adj.—v.t. improve, rectify, right, reform, better, reprove, punish, chastise, discipline, counteract, repair, neutralize. See *improvement, disapprobation.—adj.* right, regular, true, strict, accurate, exact, precise, perfect. *Ant.,* see *wrong.*

counterfeit, adj. & n.—adj. imitation, false, sham, forged, bogus, spurious. *Slang,* fake, phony.—*n.* forgery, slug, sham, brummagem, dummy, pretense. See *deception, falsehood. Ant.,* see *truth.*

1. An antonym for *correct* may be found by looking for the entry word

   _____.

2. *Counterfeit* can be used as a

   _____ or an

   _____.

3. Some slang words for *counterfeit* are

   _____ and

   _____.

4. _____ is a word one might use to describe the action of correcting a broken bicycle.

5. One might find more synonyms for *correct* by looking for the word

   _____ or

   _____.

6. The word *brummagem,* meaning *cheap* or *inferior,* is a synonym for the entry word

   _____.

Use the thesaurus entries above. Write two appropriate synonyms for each underlined word or words to give the sentence the same or similar meaning.

1. This is the <u>precise</u> spot where the accident occurred.

   _____ _____

2. The dress was a <u>phony</u>.

   _____ _____

3. I think we <u>set it right</u> eventually.

   _____ _____

4. Her cheerfulness was a <u>pretense</u>.

   _____ _____

A thesaurus stretches your word power.

Walter Hunt and the Safety Pin

Libraries have special reference books to help you locate special kinds of information. Two of these books are atlases and almanacs. In this lesson, you will learn how to use atlases and almanacs as you read about Walter Hunt, the inventor of a common object.

 ## KEYS to Using Atlases and Almanacs

Atlases are books of maps and almanacs are books of facts.

LEARN An atlas is a book of maps. The maps use words, pictures, and symbols to tell about places in the world.

An almanac is a book of facts, often in list form. Most almanacs are published every year, so the facts are up-to-date.

DIRECTIONS Tell whether you would look in an atlas or an almanac to find answers to these questions. Write *atlas* or *almanac* on the line.

1. What is the tallest building in the world?

   _____

2. What countries are in Europe?

   _____

3. Who invented the wristwatch?

   _____

4. What are the names of the provinces of Canada?

   _____

LEARN   Maps in atlases show different things. Some show cities, towns, roads and highways. Others show geographical formations like mountains, rivers, lakes, and deserts. Some may show the major products and industries of a country or region. Maps often have legends with symbols. These symbols help you locate specific items on the maps.

DIRECTIONS   Study the map of Italy, which shows important products and industries. Look at the symbols in the legend. Use the information to answer the questions and write your answers on the lines.

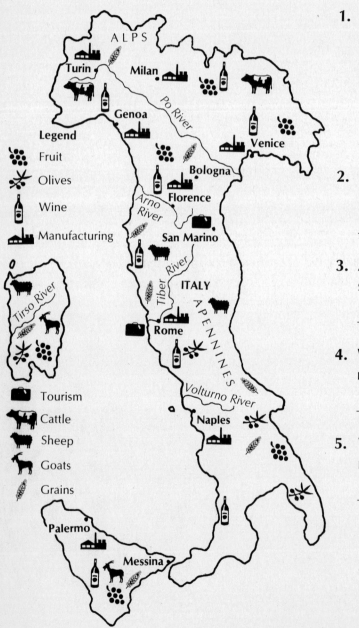

1. What products do you see in the part of Italy that is north of a line that might be drawn between Genoa and Bologna?

   _____

   _____

2. Near what two cities do you see the symbol for tourism?

   _____

3. Are olives raised in the northern or southern part of Italy?

   _____

4. What three kinds of livestock are raised in Italy?

   _____

5. Which kind of livestock is raised mostly in northern Italy?

   _____

Legend

🍇 Fruit

❋ Olives

🍾 Wine

🏭 Manufacturing

🐑 (Sardinia)

💼 Tourism

🐂 Cattle

🐑 Sheep

🐐 Goats

🌾 Grains

3 Read and Apply

DIRECTIONS Read about Walter Hunt, an inventor from the last century, and how he invented a practical little gadget called the safety pin.

Walter Hunt was a full-time inventor. His only trouble was that he never made much money from his inventions. Born in the state of New York in 1796, Hunt had, by the time he was twenty, invented a machine for spinning flax. After receiving a patent for this machine, he opened a plant to manufacture it in New York City. Unfortunately, the business failed.

Not to be discouraged, Hunt continued to think up new ideas. His next invention was an iron alarm gong that could be used on streetcars and in fire and police stations. This invention was followed by a steam table for restaurants, a knife sharpener, a coal stove called the Globe stove, an icebreaker boat, a nail-making machine, a self-closing inkwell, a fountain pen, and suction shoes that acrobats could use to walk on ceilings.

Even though most of Hunt's inventions worked, he always seemed to owe people money. One morning in 1849, he was trying to figure out how to pay a fifteen-dollar debt to a friend who had made some drawings for him. He began to fiddle with a piece of wire lying on his work table. As he bent the wire into various shapes, he suddenly had a new brainstorm. If the wire were coiled at one end and shielded at the other, it could be used as a pin that would not jab—a safety pin! Hunt applied for a patent for the safety pin that very same day. He also sold the idea for $400 and paid his debt. Then he went back to inventing.

One of Hunt's later inventions was a disposable paper collar. Unfortunately, it did not become popular until after his death in 1859. Had Hunt been a better businessman, he probably would have become a rich man. Perhaps, though, he was happiest doing what he seemed to do best—creating ideas and then transforming them into realities.

Here is part of a list of inventors and inventions that might be found in an almanac. Use the list to answer the questions.

INVENTION	INVENTOR	YEAR PATENTED
Ball point pen	John Loud	1888
Cosmetics	George Washington Carver	1925
Ironing Board	Sarah Boone	1892
Microphone	Emile Berliner	1880
Motion Picture Projector	Thomas A. Edison	1892
Phonograph	Thomas A. Edison	1877
Speaking Telegraph	Thomas A. Edison	1892
Suspenders	Samuel Clemens (Mark Twain)	1871
Videotape Recorder	Charles P. Ginsburg	1960
	Shelby Anderson, Jr.	
	Ray M. Dolby	

1. Who invented cosmetics?

_____

2. When was the motion picture projector invented?

_____

3. What did Sarah Boone invent?

_____

4. Which was invented first, the microphone or the ball point pen?

_____

5. When did Mark Twain invent suspenders?

_____

6. For which three inventions is Thomas A. Edison famous?

_____

_____

7. How many people invented the videotape recorder?

_____

REMEMBER Atlases contain maps, while almanacs contain lists of up-to-date facts on many subjects.

Special Aids in Dictionaries and Encyclopedias

You have probably used dictionaries and encyclopedias many times. You know that dictionaries have meanings and pronunciations of words. You know that encyclopedias have articles about a variety of subjects. These two reference books have other features that can help you find information. In this lesson, you will learn about some of the special aids in dictionaries and encyclopedias.

1 KEYS to Special Aids in Reference Books

Most dictionaries and encyclopedias have special features to help you find information.

LEARN   In addition to words, meanings, and pronunciations, dictionaries have other information. Most include synonyms and antonyms. Most also list prefixes and suffixes, as well as abbreviations. In addition, many dictionaries have special sections.

Encyclopedias are good reference books to use when you want an overview. It is not always easy to find what you are looking for in an encyclopedia. It helps to know how to use the index.

Another part of an encyclopedia that many people are unaware of is its year-to-date information about current events and recent discoveries.

DIRECTIONS   Complete the following sentences by filling in the blanks.

1. Most dictionaries also list prefixes, suffixes, and

   _____ .

2. An encyclopedia _____
   gives you up-to-date information.

DIRECTIONS Some dictionaries have special sections located after their main word listing. There may be a geographical section that lists the countries of the world and their capitals, as well as major cities, towns, and rivers. There may be a biographical section that lists the names and a few facts about well-known people. A dictionary might have a section that lists commonly heard foreign words and phrases, or a section that lists colleges and universities.

Assume that you are using a dictionary that has these special sections located after the main listing of words: *Biography, Foreign Words and Phrases, Geography,* and *Colleges and Universities.*

On the line after each question, tell which section you would use to find the answer.

1. When was the poet Carl Sandburg born?

   _____

   _____

2. What does the Latin phrase *id est* mean?

   _____

   _____

3. Where is Purdue University located?

   _____

   _____

4. How long is the Yukon River?

   _____

   _____

5. What is the capital of Iran?

   _____

   _____

6. Who was John Marshall?

   _____

   _____

7. What do the French words *bon soir* mean?

   _____

   _____

8. When was Lake Forest College founded?

   _____

   _____

3 Read and Apply

DIRECTIONS Read about encyclopedia indexes and yearbooks and how they can help you locate information.

Sometimes it is hard to locate a topic in an encyclopedia. For example, if you wanted to get information about *cave men,* you might search in the C volumes of several encyclopedias and find no article under that heading. One encyclopedia may have information about cave men under a topic called *prehistoric man.* Another might use the title *evolution of man.*

You can save time if you go directly to the INDEX of an encyclopedia. Usually the index is a separate volume at the end of the other volumes in the set. The index alphabetically lists all the subjects included in the encyclopedia. It also "cross-indexes;" that is, it refers the user from a *possible* topic heading to the *actual* topic heading used in that encyclopedia. If you look up "cave men," the index would probably list "cave men" and then say "see *prehistoric man,*" or "see *evolution of man.*"

Another important thing the index does is to tell you all the places in the encyclopedia (volumes and page numbers) where a subject is discussed, and under what topic headings. This is called "cross-referencing," and it helps you get the information you are looking for.

Because they are very expensive to publish, new editions of encyclopedias are not printed very frequently. Instead, most encyclopedias publish Yearbooks where readers can get up-to-date information on subjects such as current events, medicine, and health. If, for instance, you wanted to find out about political affairs of the last year in Mexico, you would consult the current yearbook. Similarly, the current yearbook would have information on the most recent discoveries in medical research. Yearbooks have their own indexes.

1. You want to find information about games of the American Indians. You have looked in the <u>G</u> volume of an encyclopedia and cannot find it there. Where should you look next?

   a. in another encyclopedia

   b. in the yearbook

   c. in the index

2. You want to find out about the latest discoveries in space exploration. Which of these would help you?

   a. special section of a dictionary

   b. encyclopedia yearbook

   c. encyclopedia index

3. You want to know what <u>COD</u> means. Where would you look?

   a. in a dictionary

   b. in an atlas

   c. in an encyclopedia

4. You need to write a report on the ten most important news events in your country during the past year. Which of these would you use?

   a. today's newspaper

   b. an encyclopedia index

   c. an encyclopedia yearbook

5. You are trying to think of a synonym for the world "build." Which of these would help you?

   a. an almanac

   b. an encyclopedia index

   c. a dictionary

6. An encyclopedia index is the first place you should look if you want to find:

   a. information about animal babies

   b. an antonym for lovely

   c. the meaning of the prefix omni

REMEMBER The special features of both encyclopedias and dictionaries are valuable reference aids.

Order in the Court

Who and what is the Supreme Court of the United States? In this lesson, you'll read about the judicial branch of the U.S. government as you learn about taking notes.

 KEYS to Notetaking

Notes are the main words of important ideas and details.

LEARN   Notes are a brief summary of important ideas and details. To take notes, read a paragraph or two and then write an important word or phrase to summarize the main idea. Write a word or phrase to help you remember any important detail.

EXAMPLE   The highest court in the United States is the Supreme Court. The task of the judicial branch of the U.S. government is to interpret laws.

Notes in List Form:

    Supreme Court (main idea)
    —Judicial branch of government (detail)
    —Interprets laws (detail)

DIRECTIONS Read the paragraph. Use the underlined words to complete the notes in list form below.

  The <u>Supreme Court</u> consists of nine judges, or justices. <u>Eight</u> of the judges are <u>associate justices</u>, and <u>one</u> judge is the <u>chief justice</u>.

Notes: _____ (main idea)

   —

    _____ (detail)

   —

    _____ (detail)

Practice Notetaking

DIRECTIONS To sort out the main idea and details of a paragraph, it is helpful to find brief answers to the basic questions *who or what, when, why, how,* and *where.* Answers to some or all of these questions will help you create notes. Read the paragraph. Use the underlined words to answer the questions below. The first one is done for you.

The Supreme Court of the United States is the only court created by the Constitution. The purpose of the Supreme Court was to guarantee equal justice to all people in America. Officially established in 1789, the first court met in New York City in a building called the Royal Exchange.

A. Who or what? Supreme Court _____

B. When? _____

C. Why? _____
_____

D. How? _____
_____

E. Where? _____

DIRECTIONS After noting the main ideas and details of a paragraph, it is helpful to organize the notes into an outline. Use the phrases you wrote above to complete the outline.

I. _____
   A. Where and when established?
      1. _____
         _____
      2. _____
         _____

   B. Why and how established?
      1. _____
         _____
      2. _____
         _____

3 Read and Apply

DIRECTIONS Notes may be taken in various forms. If lists of dates or other facts are being noted, a chart or table might best organize the data. Read the paragraph and the notes that follow.

Chief Justice William H. Rehnquist was appointed to the Supreme Court in 1972 by Richard Nixon. Nixon also appointed Justice Harry A. Blackmun in 1970, and Justice Lewis F. Powell, Jr. in 1972. Dwight D. Eisenhower recommended the appointment of William J. Brennan, Jr. to the court in 1956, while Justice Byron R. White was selected in 1962 by John F. Kennedy. Gerald R. Ford's selection of Justice John P. Stevens in 1975 preceded Ronald Reagan's choice in 1981 of Sandra Day O'Connor as the first female to serve on the United States Supreme Court. In 1987 Justice Powell resigned and Anthony Kennedy was appointed early in 1988.

Notes in Table Form:

Present Supreme Court Justices

Name	Term	Appointed by
William J. Brennan, Jr.	1956	Eisenhower
Byron R. White	1962	Kennedy
Thurgood Marshall	1967	Johnson
Harry A. Blackmun	1970	Nixon
William H. Rehnquist	1972	Nixon
John P. Stevens	1975	Ford
Sandra Day O'Connor	1981	Reagan
Antonin Scalia	1986	Reagan
Anthony Kennedy	1988	Reagan

DIRECTIONS Cause-and-effect relationships can be noted as a diagram by drawing an arrow from the cause words to the effect words. Read the paragraph and the notes in diagram form.

When a member of the Supreme Court dies or retires, the president recommends a candidate to fill the vacancy. The person's background and experience are investigated by the Senate before a justice is officially appointed.

Notes in Diagram Form:

New Justice

vacancy ⟶ president ⟶ candidate ⟶ Senate ⟶ appointment

Read each paragraph. Then use the underlined words to complete the notes in the suggested form below.

A. Although <u>many cases</u> are presented to the <u>Supreme Court</u>, it is not obligated to consider every case. It selects only those <u>cases</u> which involve <u>issues</u> of <u>national</u> importance.

Diagram:

_____ $\longrightarrow$ _____ $\longrightarrow$ _____

B. The Supreme Court meets in the <u>Supreme Court Building</u> in <u>Washington, D.C.</u> The work year commences the <u>first Monday in October</u>, and the court normally <u>recesses in June</u>.

Outline: Supreme Court

I. Where it meets

  A. _____

  B. _____

    _____

II. When it meets

  A. _____

    _____

  B. _____

C. Several Supreme Court Justices have made major contributions in history. <u>John Marshall</u>, appointed in <u>1801</u>, is credited with a decision that the Supreme Court could <u>discard laws</u> made by Congress if the laws were against the Constitution. <u>In 1902</u>, <u>Oliver Wendell Holmes</u> joined the Supreme Court and successfully argued that <u>laws should change</u> as the needs of people change. The first chief justice, <u>John Jay</u>, was appointed in <u>1790</u>. Justice Jay was instrumental in drawing up a <u>treaty</u> to end hard feelings between the United States and England.

Chart: Major Contributions of Justices

Name	Appointed	Contribution
_____	_____	_____
_____	_____	_____
_____	_____	_____

REMEMBER Notetaking organizes important ideas and details.

Feline Facts

What do you know about cats? In this lesson, you'll read some feline facts as you learn about a special way to take notes.

 KEYS to Notetaking

Write main ideas and details in an organized way.

LEARN   *Note Maps* resemble diagrams. The main idea is at the top or center. Subtopics are in boxes connected to the main idea. Details are connected to the subtopic they explain.

EXAMPLE

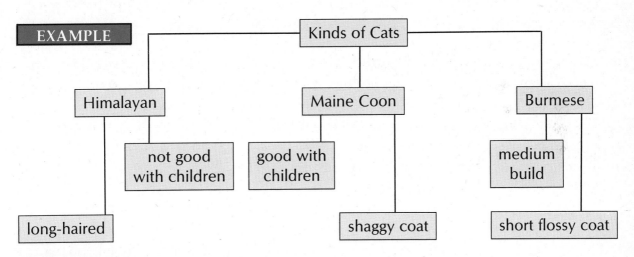

DIRECTIONS   Answer the questions.

1. What is the main idea? _____

2. What two details describe Burmese cats?

_____   _____

3. What are the three subtopics?

_____   _____   _____

Practice Notetaking

DIRECTIONS Read each paragraph and complete the map below it.

A. There are several types of purebred cats. An Abyssinian looks like a miniature cougar. Its coat is soft and easy to care for. Abyssinians are gentle, playful, and very intelligent. The Persian cat, although gentle, is not a lap cat, since it dislikes being held. A Persian's long hair requires constant grooming.

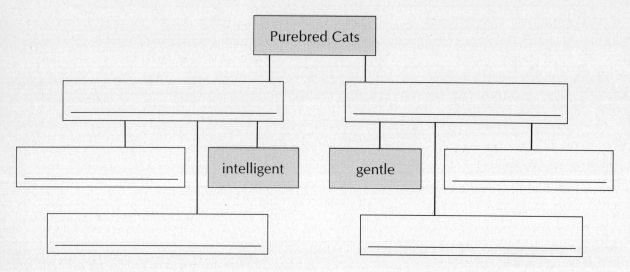

B. The Russian Blue, another purebred cat, has an exceedingly quiet nature. Affectionate and loyal, this short-haired cat has silver-tipped hairs. In contrast to the Russian Blue, the blue-eyed Siamese is anything but quiet! Though temperamental, Siamese cats are very social and bask in human companionship. A naturally lively cat, the Manx has a double coat and no tail.

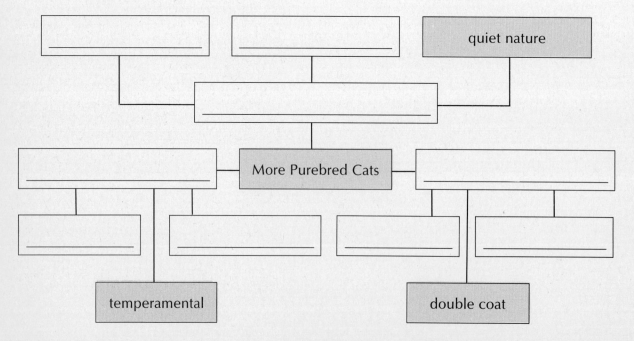

Read and Apply

Read about some parasites that bother cats.

Cats are troubled by internal and external parasites, or creatures that survive by feeding off other creatures.

Some common external parasites found on cats are ear mites, mange mites, fleas, ticks, and lice. All these pests cause severe itching, skin infections, and if left untreated, loss of hair.

Fleas are tiny brown insects that live on the cat's skin and survive by sucking the animal's blood. Although they cannot fly, fleas travel easily by jumping from place to place. Like fleas, ticks suck a cat's blood. They bury their heads into the skin. Fleas can be found anywhere on a cat's body, but they prefer the head area around the ears.

Lice are tiny insects without wings. Barely visible to the human eye, cat lice live only on cats and can't survive on dogs or humans. Also miniscule in size and particular about where they live, mange mites spend all their short lives on the animal. Ear mites resemble mange mites in size but live primarily in the ear canals of cats.

The most common internal parasites that plague cats are roundworms, hookworms, tapeworms, heartworms, toxoplasmosis, and coccidia.

Hookworms are more commonly found in the intestines of young kittens than in older cats. An examination is necessary to detect the small parasites that are less than a half-inch long. Roundworms, also commonly found in kittens, are long and white and resemble spaghetti. Because roundworms can infect humans, this parasite is considered a public health hazard.

Tapeworms are flat and resemble pieces of tape or grains of rice. As cats groom themselves, they may swallow fleas which have tapeworm infestation. The flea is digested, and the tapeworm eggs are released in the cat's intestine.

Heartworm, only seen in dogs until recent years, can be transmitted to cats by mosquitoes. The worm lives in the right side of a cat's heart and can be fatal if untreated.

Unlike the worm-type parasites, coccidia are one-celled organisms that dwell in a cat's intestines. Very young kittens are most susceptible to coccidia. The coccidia is often found where many kittens are housed in unsanitary conditions.

Toxoplasmosis, also a one-celled protozoan parasite, can be found in many warm-blooded animals, but completes its life cycle only in the intestines of cats. The parasite is contracted when cats eat raw meat.

DIRECTIONS Use the article you just read to complete the map about internal and external parasites.

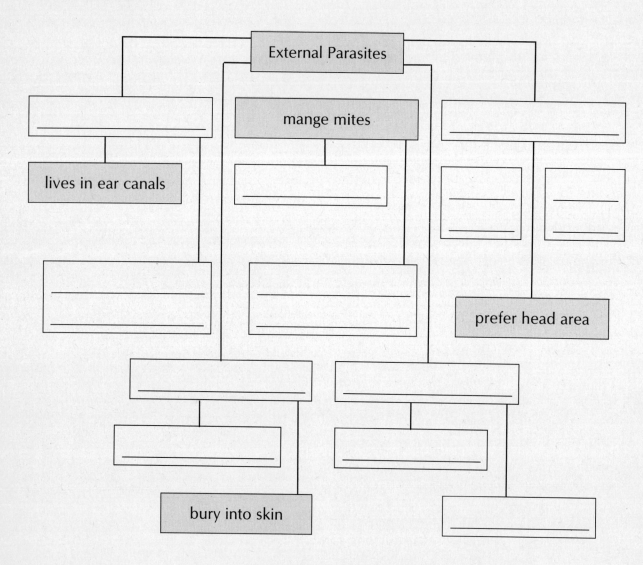

REMEMBER Mapping is a helpful form of notetaking.

Cash or Charge?

How do people pay for purchases? In this lesson, you'll read about banks, money, and making purchases as you learn about outlining.

 KEYS to Outlining

Outlining is a useful way to organize information.

LEARN Main ideas in an outline are preceded by *Roman numerals*. *Capital letters* denote subtopics, and details follow *Arabic numerals*. Main ideas are explained by subtopics, while details tell more about subtopics.

EXAMPLE

I. Federal Reserve System
  A. Definition
    1. Twelve banks
    2. Holder of money reserves
  B. Purposes
    1. Watches over banks
    2. Issues emergency loans to banks

DIRECTIONS Read each sentence. Then use the above outline as you write *main idea, subtopic,* or *detail* on the line to identify the sentences the notes were taken from.

_____ **1.** One purpose of the Federal Reserve Bank is to *issue emergency loans to banks* when necessary.

_____ **2.** The *Federal Reserve System* consists of special banks throughout the United States.

_____ **3.** The Federal Reserve System has two important *purposes*.

2 Practice Outlining

DIRECTIONS Read about banks. Then complete the outline below.

A bank is a place that holds people's money in safekeeping for later use or for savings. Banks keep in reserve a small part of the money people deposit, or put into the bank. Banks then use the rest of the deposit to make loans to others or to invest to earn interest. People deposit money into a checking account in a bank and then write checks. A check is a written instruction for the bank to pay out some of the money from a person's checking account.

There are several different kinds of banks. An independent bank is a local bank which accepts deposits in checking and savings accounts. Independent banks have no branches, or banks by the same name, in other locations. Commercial banks also handle checking accounts, but specialize in helping businesses by making loans to them.

National banks are commercial banks. The federal government licenses, or gives permission, for national banks to operate. Because national banks are chartered by the federal government, they are considered members of the Federal Reserve System.

Federal Reserve Banks are also part of the Federal Reserve System. These banks hold the majority of the reserve funds kept by all other banks when deposits are made. Banks that are part of the Federal Reserve System do not operate to make a profit like other kinds of banks. Instead, the Federal Reserve Banks watch over and help other banks.

I. Banks _____

  A. Purpose of Banks _____

    1. _____

       _____

    2. _____

       _____

    3. _____

       _____

  B. _____

    1. _____

    2. _____

    3. National _____

II. _____

  A. What It Is _____

    1. _____

       _____

    2. _____

       _____

  B. What It Does _____

    1. _____

       _____

    2. _____

       _____

DIRECTIONS Read about options for buying goods and services.

It is common today, when making a purchase, to be asked, "Cash or charge?" Cash purchases may be made with currency or by check. Currency means paper bills and coins, whereas a check is a paper document which represents cash. To pay by check, a person must have a checking account in a bank. When money is deposited in a bank to open a checking account, the bank issues a book of checks.

When a check is written and signed by the owner of the checking account, the person is authorizing the bank to pay out some of their deposited money. The payer, or person writing the check, is paying money to the payee, or person receiving the check. The payee generally requires a form of identification, such as a driver's license, to prove that the payer is the owner of the checking account. The payee then endorses, or signs the back of the check, and presents it to the bank in exchange for the amount of currency written on the check.

Another way to make a purchase is to "charge" by using a credit or charge card. The first credit card was issued in 1959 in California. Since that time, "charging" has become a popular and convenient way of making purchases. A credit card represents agreement by the buyer to "buy now and pay later" and the bank or business's willingness to loan money.

Plastic credit cards are issued by banks, department stores, airlines, gasoline companies, and other businesses. A person borrows money by using the credit card to purchase goods or services. *Goods* are products such as clothing, books, or other such items. *Services* are duties performed by people, such as the repair of a bicycle or the lesson given by a music or gymnastics expert. A purchase may include goods and services, such as when a bicycle requires a new part to be properly repaired. The part is goods, and the repair is a service.

To obtain a credit card, a person must complete a form and sign an agreement to repay the costs of any purchases made by using the credit card. The repayment may be made in full or in installments, which means paying a small amount of the balance each month until the total loan is repaid. A bank, store, or other business charges an *interest* fee which pays for their willingness to wait until later to receive their cash.

People use credit cards for convenience. They may not have cash or

enough money in a checking account to make a purchase when an item or service is wanted or needed. The buyer must be confident, however, that the cash will be available soon to repay the credit-card loan.

Using a credit card is a convenient way to make purchases when traveling, since a check may not be accepted in a location far from a person's local bank. Carrying a large amount of cash when traveling can be bulky, and the cash may be lost or stolen. Some people use charge cards in order to have a record of their purchases. Others may prefer to charge purchases in order to make one monthly payment rather than spend smaller amounts of money at a time during the month.

Being reasonable is crucial when using credit cards. Buyers must practice self-control to avoid spending more money than they can afford to pay when repayment is due.

DIRECTIONS Complete the partial outline of the article you just read.

Making a Purchase

I. Ways To Pay _____

   A. _____

      1. _____

      2. _____

   B. _____

      1. _____

      2. _____

      3. Buy now and pay later _____

II. Kinds of Purchases _____

   A. _____

   B. _____

III. Reasons for Charging _____

   A. _____

   B. _____

   C. _____

   D. _____

REMEMBER Outlining organizes main ideas, subtopics, and details.

Every Dog Should Own a Human

When you find information to use in a report, you need to rewrite it in your own words. In this lesson, you'll learn to state the ideas you read in your own words. You'll also read about some interesting role-reversals.

 ## KEYS to Paraphrasing

Paraphrasing is writing ideas in your own words.

LEARN   To *paraphrase* something you read, rewrite the main idea in your own words. Use synonyms for the author's main words, and rearrange the information.

EXAMPLE   *Original:* My owners frequently stretch my patience to the limit as they question the rules I set for them.
Paraphrased: My humans are forever challenging the rules I establish around this house.

DIRECTIONS   Read each pair of sentences. Circle the words in sentence *b* that are substituted for the underlined words in sentence *a*.

a. Humans should <u>consult</u> their dogs <u>before</u> making plans for an evening out.

b. If humans want to go out, they have to ask their dogs first.

a. An <u>individual's well-stated opinion</u> can <u>affect</u> the <u>direction</u> of the <u>whole group</u>.

b. One person's feeling, if spoken carefully, can change the actions of many.

② Practice Paraphrasing

DIRECTIONS The goal of paraphrasing a paragraph is to take the main idea and restate it in one or two sentences. Read the steps of paraphrasing. Then read the brief article and complete the work below.

1. Read a few paragraphs of an article.

2. Stop reading and record the important ideas in a few words or phrases.

3. Reread the passage and add to or correct your notes.

4. Continue steps 1, 2, and 3 as you read the whole article.

5. Select the most important words and phrases in your notes.

6. Restate the main ideas in your own words. Omit unnecessary words.

7. Rewrite each main idea in one or two sentences.

8. Reread and rewrite or rearrange the sentences as necessary.

Yesterday surging river waters poured over protective sandbags and flooded the residences of Lake Road Lagoons. The waters left more than thirty families homeless, and the entire area was without electrical service.

Hardest hit were the river-edge homes near the Left Bank Yacht Club. Homeowners told stories of extensive damage to house furnishings and complained about the inability to get insurance to cover such a disaster.

The river continues to rise, and more flooding is expected. Homeless residents are being accommodated in the area's churches and schools.

1. Write words or phrases to tell the main idea of each paragraph.

    a. _____

    b. _____

    c. _____

2. Rewrite each main idea in your own words.

    a. _____

    _____

    b. _____

    _____

    c. _____

DIRECTIONS Look for main ideas as you read the article.

Every dog should have a human of his own. There is nothing like a well-behaved person around the house to spread the dog's blanket for him or bring him his supper when he comes home human-tired at night. Properly trained, a human can be a dog's best friend.

I happen to belong to a medium-sized English setter, who acquired me when he was about six months old and has been training me quite successfully ever since. He has taught me to shake hands with him and fetch his ball. I've learned not to tug at the leash when he takes me for a walk, and I make him a devoted companion. In fact, my setter has broken me so thoroughly that I have decided to set down a few of his basic rules of human-handling, as a guide for other dogs.

The first problem for a dog is to pick out the right human. A dog should exercise great care in making his choice, since he is apt to become quite attached to the human and will find it hard to get rid of him later if he proves unsatisfactory.

The next question for a dog to decide is whether he and the human should share the house together. Some dogs prefer a kennel, but others decide to move right in the house. In the latter case, it's especially important to establish boundaries for the human from the start. If a dog prefers the big over-stuffed chair in the living room, he needs to let the human know in no uncertain terms that the chair is taken.

It is a great mistake for a dog to break a human by using force. Punishment should be used rarely, and then only in cases of deliberate disobedience. More can be accomplished by a reproachful look than by a fit of temper. A dog doesn't need to raise a paw. He can cure a human of the habit of running away by simply lying down on the floor with his chin in his forepaws and gazing sadly. Most humans will eventually unpack the suitcases and turn in the train reservations.

In training a human, diet is very important. The average human has a tendency to gobble everything in sight. The dog should exercise a restraining influence by eating all the leftovers in the house before the human gets a chance at them.

Last but not least, it is up to the dog to see that his human has the right com-

panions. If the dog does not approve of a guest who has been invited to the house, he should express his dislike by removing a small section of the visitor's trouser leg as a gentle hint.

Training a human takes time, of course. A dog should realize that a human does not possess a dog's instincts, and it is not the human's fault when the dog's desires are misunderstood. Humans are apt to be high-strung and sensitive, and a dog who loses his temper will only break the human's spirit. A dog must be patient and understanding, and not fly off the handle if his human cannot learn to chase rabbits. After all, it's hard to teach an old human new tricks.

DIRECTIONS Read each sentence. Use synonyms as you rearrange the information to write the sentence in your own words.

1. It's up to the dog to see that his human has the right companions.

_____

_____

2. A dog should realize that a human does not possess a dog's instincts.

_____

_____

3. A dog must be patient and understanding, and not fly off the handle if his human cannot learn to chase rabbits.

_____

_____

DIRECTIONS Write a three-or-four-sentence paragraph to paraphrase the main idea of the article about a dog owning a human.

_____

_____

_____

_____

_____

_____

REMEMBER Capture important ideas in your own words.

Matters of Money

What was the *Great Depression?* What is *inflation?* In this lesson, you'll read about depression, inflation, and other matters of concern in the field of economics. You'll also learn about writing reports.

1 KEYS to Report Writing

A report is written from an outline and organized notes.

LEARN The first step in writing a report is to locate information on your topic. Books and magazine articles are excellent sources, as is an encyclopedia. Next, read information from three, four, or more sources and take notes to summarize what you've read. Then organize your notes into groups and arrange the main topics in the order you will use in the report. Finally, you'll make an outline of each main topic with its subtopics and details.

DIRECTIONS Write a word on the line to complete each statement.

1. I will take notes from at least _____ different sources of information.

2. I'll use my notes to write an _____ of main topics, subtopics, and details.

3. I need to _____ my notes by topic.

4. My notes will summarize the _____ I read.

5. An _____ must not be my only source of information.

6. As I sort my notes, I'll decide the order I'll present the _____ in my report.

2 Practice Report Writing

DIRECTIONS An outline and organized notes provide a guide for writing a report. Each main idea in the outline represents the idea for a paragraph's topic sentence. Read the outline and notes collected on the topic of the Law of Supply and Demand. Then read and complete the sentences below to tell the things you do in writing a report.

Money Matters
I Law of Supply and Demand
  A. Supply
    1. Amount of goods and services available
    2. Usually goes up as prices go up
  B. Demand
    1. Amount of things people want to buy
    2. Usually goes down as prices go up

Notes on Supply and Demand
— higher prices encourage more production
— lower prices discourage production
— called a law because it can be relied on to happen
— goods are things like cars, clothes, and toys
— services are duties performed, like giving lessons or repairing things

---

1. The main topic is _____, which will be the first paragraph of my report.

2. In my first paragraph, I'll write a sentence or two about why the topic is called a _____.

3. My second paragraph will be about the meaning of the first subtopic word which is _____.

4. I'll use the details under the first _____ and my notes to write about the meaning of _____.

5. My third paragraph will be about the meaning of the second _____ which is _____.

6. I'll use the _____ under the second subtopic, along with my _____, to write about the meaning of _____.

Read and Apply

DIRECTIONS Read the partial outline and the notes about *inflation* from several sources. Then complete the paragraphs below as they might be written in a report on money matters.

Money Matters

II *Inflation*
    A. *Causes*
        1. *Spending exceeds saving*
        2. *More money than goods and services*
    B. *Results*
        1. *Prices go up*
        2. *People can't buy things*

Inflation Notes

— *people hurry to buy things in fear of prices going up*
— *demand for things is high*
— *supply of things is low*
— *prices rise quickly*
— *banks short of money*
— *people aren't saving*
— *people spend more than save*
— *too much money in circulation*

My Report

Inflation happens when people are

_____ more money

than they _____ .

Too much _____

is then in circulation. There is more

_____ than there

are _____ and

_____ to be

purchased.

    When inflation occurs, the

_____ of goods

and services _____ .

As prices increase, people hurry

out to _____ things

because they fear prices will

_____ even more

later. The demand for things is then

_____ and often

goes higher as the supply of things

becomes _____ .

Then people are unable to

_____ the things

they want.

Read the partial outline and the two forms of notes taken from readings about the Great Depression. Write two paragraphs about the Great Depression on the lines.

Notes on Great Depression
- started in 1929
- continued into 1930s
- people unable to buy
- no money in banks
- people unable to pay on bank loans
- people wanted to take their savings from banks
- money scarce
- businesses stopped producing goods
- workers lost jobs

Money Matters
III The Great Depression
  A. When
    1. 1929 2. Continued into 1930's
  B. What
    1. Great recession or slowdown
    2. People lost jobs
    3. Businesses failed
    4. Money scarce

Notes Diagram

People stop buying.
↓
Stores buy less merchandise.
↓
Manufacturers produce less.
↓
Businesses that supply factories fail.
↓
Jobs are scarce.
↓
People have no money.

_____

_____

_____

_____

_____

_____

_____

_____

_____

An outline and organized notes make report writing easy.

It's Debatable

Why would anyone suggest taking a dog to a psychologist? In this lesson, you'll read some pros and cons of this issue and others as you learn about debating.

 1 **KEYS to Debating**

Facts must support each position in a debate.

LEARN An *issue* is a problem or concern. An issue is *debated* when opposing opinions are expressed. One side is in favor of an issue, and the other side is against it. Each side states its position, then presents facts to support that position. A panel of judges listens to both arguments and decides which side has presented the most convincing facts.

EXAMPLE Issue: Should allowances require the performance of chores?
In favor: Allowances should be given according to chores performed.
Against: Chores should not be required in order to receive an allowance.

DIRECTIONS Write *in favor* or *against* on the line before each statement to show which position the argument supports.

_____ **1.** An allowance should be given to teach children to use money wisely.

_____ **2.** An allowance should be increased when more chores are added.

_____ **3.** When chores aren't done, no allowance should be given.

_____ **4.** Children shouldn't be paid to do chores.

KEYS to Debating

DIRECTIONS To support a position in a debate, you need to read about the issue and then organize convincing facts. Read each question and the position statements. Then read each sentence below and write *1* or *2* on the line to show which position the sentence supports.

A. Should children be allowed to read as late as they like before falling asleep at night?

1. Children should be allowed to read as long as they like at night before going to sleep.

2. Parents should set a time when lights are to be out at night.

_____ **a.** Reading before going to sleep is relaxing.

_____ **b.** Some children can't fall asleep right away.

_____ **c.** Curfews or "lights out" are necessary for children.

_____ **d.** A day's end is more pleasurable if one is allowed to read until sleepy.

_____ **e.** Some children would read all night if allowed.

B. Should television viewing time be limited for children?

1. The amount of television-viewing time should be pre-determined for children.

2. Children should be allowed to watch television as much as they like.

_____ **a.** Children will carefully select their choices if given a time limit.

_____ **b.** Because children have many interests, they won't sit and watch television all day.

_____ **c.** Many TV shows aren't interesting to children, so they choose other activities.

_____ **d.** Children need help in balancing their time between active and inactive activities.

_____ **e.** Watching TV can be habit-forming.

DIRECTIONS Look for facts that support opposing positions as you read about a possible solution for a problem pet.

"What a crazy idea!" said George. "You need an obedience school. Dog's don't go to psychologists!"

"Wait a minute, George!" said Jake. "Maybe we should hear what Tina has to say. What do you know about this animal psychology stuff, Tina?"

"Well, my parents and I have tried everything we can think of with Ralphie. He destroys anything in sight whenever he hears thunder."

"We've read articles about how psychologists work with animals," continued Tina. "It's becoming more popular because people really treasure their pets and aren't willing to give them up when a problem arises. Psychologists work with dogs that do strange things like Ralphie does. Therapy is also recommended for a dog that bites or one that goes berserk when a truck or car approaches. We've read that some problems aren't appropriate for therapy. A dog that sometimes barks too much or occasionally has an accident in the house probably needs obedience school rather than therapy. A dog that attacks its owner, though, can be helped in therapy."

"Animal psychologists cost a lot of money!" chimed T.J. "I read that it's at least $50 an hour! That's too much to spend on an animal."

"Not if you love your pet," said Tina. "It's estimated that 75% of the cases are treatable and just a few hours of therapy usually show dramatic results."

"I love my cat, but I think I'd trust my vet's advice," said Jake. "Her fees aren't nearly as high, either. Everything I've read says that giving affection to your pet is most important. All an owner needs to do is be stern when the pet disobeys or acts strange."

"Well, we think therapy is worth a try. I'll keep you posted on Ralphie's progress."

DIRECTIONS Use the story you just read to complete each statement. Circle the letter of the correct answer.

1. The issue is
   a. whether to seek therapy for a problem pet.
   b. whether to give away a problem pet.
   c. whether to take a pet to obedience school.
   d. none of the above.

2. Tina's position is that
   a. therapy is too expensive.
   b. therapy is not appropriate for Ralphie's problem.
   c. animals can benefit from therapy.
   d. animals should not go to therapy.

3. The position taken by George and T.J. is that
   a. animals should not go to psychologists.
   b. a problem pet can't ever be helped.
   c. animals cannot benefit from obedience school.
   d. therapy is a good idea for animals.

DIRECTIONS Read each position statement. Then write facts from the story to support each position. Write your own opinion on the lines below.

1. Animals with problems should be taken to animal psychologists for therapy:

   a. _____

   b. _____

   _____

   d. _____

2. Problem animals should not be taken to animal psychologists for treatment:

   a. _____

   b. _____

   c. _____

   d. _____

My opinion on this issue is: _____

_____

REMEMBER Debating requires supporting facts.

The Question Is . . .

How "test-wise" are you? In this lesson, you'll learn about tests, types of questions on tests, and some tips for becoming more "test-wise."

 KEYS to Taking Tests

Test questions are presented in different forms.

LEARN Tests help determine which skills you have mastered and which need to be reviewed. A *pretest* shows how much you already know about new material. A *posttest* determines how well you have learned the subject matter. Test questions may be presented in one or several of the following ways:

TYPE OF QUESTION	WHAT YOU DO
Sentence completion	Supply a missing word or words.
Multiple choice	Select from several choices.
Matching	Find items that go together.
True-False	Decide whether a statement is true.
Essay	Write what you know.

The first four types are called *objective* questions, which are scored as right or wrong. Answers on *subjective* questions, like essay questions, range from totally correct to totally incorrect. You may earn partial credit for answers that are partly correct.

DIRECTIONS Write a word on the line to complete each sentence.

1. A _____ is given after subject matter is presented.

2. A true-false question is an example of an _____ test question.

② Practice Test-Taking

DIRECTIONS Read each paragraph about taking tests. Then answer the questions.

A. A true-false question must be totally true to be marked *true*. Words like *all*, *always*, *never*, *sometimes*, *only*, and *usually* are key words to consider when deciding if a statement is true or false.

 1. Test questions are always in objective form.   T   F

B. A word list may be given for sentence-completion items, or you may be required to supply the missing word from memory.

 1. A _____ determines how well subject matter is mastered.

C. Your goal in a multiple-choice question is to eliminate incorrect answers. If more than one answer is correct, you need to look for an answer which is a combination of others or "all of the above."

 1. An objective test may include

 a. multiple-choice questions.   **c.** sentence-completion items.

 b. essay questions.   **d.** both *a* and *c*.

D. Although answers are provided, matching questions require you to determine relationships in order to match items. Extra items may be given, an item may not be used, or an item may be matched to more than one other item. You may be asked to complete the matching by drawing a line, writing the complete answer, or writing the letter of the answer.

 1. Match the items by writing the letter or letters from the list at the right.

 _____ Posttests   **a.** check skill mastery.

 _____ True-false questions   **b.** may be objective or subjective.

 _____ Multiple-choice questions   **c.** do not allow for "maybe."

 _____ Objective tests   **d.** are scored as right or wrong.

E. An essay question asks you to write what you know. You may include conclusions and opinions, but you'll need to include facts that show you understand the subject matter.

 1. Discuss how objective and subjective test questions differ.

 _____

 _____

 _____

 _____

DIRECTIONS   Read about different kinds of tests and their purposes.

An achievement test measures knowledge and understanding of a particular subject. Tests to measure achievement are scored in one of two ways. A person's performance may be compared to that of others who took the test. In this case, the highest-ranking score may not be a perfect score. When tests are graded "on the curve," the total score is not 100%. It is the highest number of correctly-answered questions.

Another scoring method for achievement tests is when each person's performance is compared to a predetermined standard. In this case, a particular score is required to earn a passing grade, and a standard is established for each letter grade.

An ability test predicts how well a student can learn. Intelligence, or men-tal ability, tests include questions about information and skills which a person may have learned in many different ways. Many questions require the student to use reasoning to solve problems. Although ability tests are commonly called intelligence tests, they do not measure how smart a person is, but how well the person can use information they've learned.

Aptitude and interest tests ask questions designed to reveal a person's interests and talents. Such questions as "Do you like to work puzzles?" and "Would you rather build a model or draw a picture?" attempt to determine a person's preferred types of activities. There are no right or wrong answers on aptitude tests, since the purpose of such tests is to help people know their interests and strengths.

Many tests require you to write your answers on a separate sheet of paper. If computer scoring is used, you'll be instructed to mark the answer sheet by shading a box or making other specific marks. Be sure your marks are made neatly and firmly.

Read each statement or question. Shade the correct box on the answer sheet.

1. An achievement test reveals a person's interest. (a) T (b) F

2. A score of 90% may be required to pass a test. (a) T (b) F

3. A spelling test is an achievement test. (a) T (b) F

4. Answers on an aptitude test are scored as right or wrong. (a) T (b) F

5. All tests are scored by computers. (a) T (b) F

6. Grading "on the curve" means
   a. the highest score may not be a perfect paper.
   b. test scores are compared to each other.
   c. both *a* and *b*.
   d. neither *a* nor *b*.

7. An aptitude test
   a. measures a person's ability to learn.
   b. reveals a person's ability to solve problems.
   c. reveals what a person likes to do best.
   d. measures a person's mastery of skills.

8. An essay question
   a. requires you to supply a missing word.
   b. allows you to write the answer in your own words.
   c. is an example of an objective question.

9. Objective test questions can be
   a. multiple-choice, essay, true-false, and sentence-completion type.
   b. sentence-completion, matching, true-false, and essay type.
   c. true-false, multiple-choice, matching, and sentence-completion type.
   d. none of the above.

1. (a) (b) (c) (d)   6. (a) (b) (c) (d)
2. (a) (b) (c) (d)   7. (a) (b) (c) (d)
3. (a) (b) (c) (d)   8. (a) (b) (c) (d)
4. (a) (b) (c) (d)   9. (a) (b) (c) (d)
5. (a) (b) (c) (d)

REMEMBER Being "test-wise" helps you score well on tests.

Junk Food Junkie

Good readers change their reading speed to fit their purpose for reading. In this lesson, you will learn about different reading speeds for different purposes. You'll also learn about diets and how vegetarians have changed the foods they eat.

KEYS to Reading Rate

Each reading rate suits a purpose.

LEARN   When a passage contains many ideas and facts, you need to read more slowly. Very fast reading is handy when you're reading for an important idea or word. *Skimming* is a fast reading rate used to get a main idea. Use the "Ask-Read-Ask" hint to help you skim:

ASK: What do I want to find out?
READ: Read the important words only, while thinking about what you're trying to find out.
ASK: Have I found the information I need?

DIRECTIONS   Read the reason for reading. Then skim the paragraph and complete the work below.

Reason for reading: How are the menus of vegetarian restaurants different from menus of traditional restaurants?

   Since vegetarians do not eat meat, their diet is fruits, vegetables, seeds, nuts, and grains. Menus in vegetarian restaurants do not include hamburger, or steak. Instead, the menu would be likely to advertise soyburger specials, tofu tomato, legume and grain platters, and sauteed seasonal vegetables.

1. Do vegetarian restaurants serve meats and fried foods? _____

2. Why would you find lots of vegetables on a menu in a vegetarian restaurant?

2 Practice With Reading Rate

DIRECTIONS Another fast-reading speed is called *scanning*. Scanning helps you find specific details. To scan, you move your eyes quickly over the page as you search for a particular word, number, or idea to answer a question. When you are looking for a name or number in a phone book, you scan the page and skip most of the text. Read each reason for reading. Then scan the paragraph and complete the statement below it.

A. Reason for reading: When did Murray Rose become a vegetarian?

Murray Rose, an Australian, became a world champion swimmer and winner of the Olympic games. He was a powerful swimmer who demonstrated great strength and endurance. At the age of two, with the aid and influence of his parents, Murray became a vegetarian. His diet habits have been widely publicized.

1. Murray Rose became a vegetarian

_____ .

B. Reason for reading: What popular meat dish does Nut Roast resemble?

Nut Roast is a popular vegetarian dish. It is made of a blend of nuts and grains. Several natural herbs and vegetables are used as seasoning. The roast is baked in a pan and looks much like meatloaf. Nut Roast is often topped with gravy and served with potatoes and fresh vegetables for dinner.

1. Nut Roast resembles

_____ .

DIRECTIONS Write *skim* or *scan* on the line to tell which reading rate you'd use to answer each reason for reading.

1. What is the address of the nearest video store?

_____

2. What kind of diet habits does Murray Rose have?

_____

3. What ingredients are used to make a Nut Roast?

_____

4. What's the nature of the main character's problem?

_____

3 Read and Apply

DIRECTIONS Read the story slowly and carefully.

Dad, Vickie, and I picnicked in the backyard almost every night. Dad loved to barbecue ribs and hot dogs and hamburgers. He'd wear the silly white chef's hat Aunt Karen had given him, and he'd smoke up the entire yard. Once the neighbors called the fire department! He had just finished flipping the burgers that fateful evening in July when Vicki dropped her bean sprouts bombshell.

"Dad, Mike, I've decided to give up eating meat and become a vegetarian."

Dad didn't even look up from the grill. He was used to Vicki's ideas about health. She always nagged him to quit smoking, and she badgered me to give up soda and bubble gum. We paid as much attention to her as an elephant does to an ant. Whenever she tried to feed me "healthy" food, I gave it to the dog or dumped it in the flower bed.

"Well, Mike, I guess that means more burgers for us!" laughed Dad.

"Vicki, you must be crazy!" I shouted. "I can't stand vegetables. You're not going to turn me into a 'Cabbage Patch Kid'."

"It's too late; you're already a turkey!" snapped Vicki.

"That's enough, both of you," said Dad. "I don't want this bickering during dinner. If Vicki wants to be a vegetarian, that's fine with me as long as she gets enough protein. Mike and I can continue to eat meat. Now the matter is closed."

All summer, Vicki ate bean sprouts and tofu and cheese and beans. She read labels at the supermarket and wouldn't buy anything that had artificial ingredients. I was reduced to smuggling soda and junk food into the house, because I couldn't stand the way she glared at me whenever I ate my favorite foods.

I started to get pretty annoyed about the whole situation when I caught her mixing wheat germ into our meat loaf one night!

Use the story you just read to answer the questions.

1. What are the names of the two main characters in the story?

   _____

   _____

   _____

2. When and where does the story take place?

   _____

   _____

   _____

3. How does the older sister want the family to change?

   _____

   _____

   _____

4. What items does the younger brother eat that might upset the older sister?

   _____

   _____

   _____

5. What habit does the older sister yell at her dad about?

   _____

   _____

DIRECTIONS Read each reason for reading. Then use the correct reading rate to read the paragraph. Write your answer on the line below.

A. Reason for Reading: Do people need to eat meat in order to survive?

   SKIM: The age-old idea that humans need meat to survive is being questioned today. A large number of people have found that they stay very healthy on a diet without any meat. They eat a vegetarian diet. Whole nations of the world survive on meatless diets. Asians and Hindus, for example, eat very little meat.

   ANSWER: _____

   _____

   _____

B. Reason for Reading: What foods provide calcium?

   SCAN: Calcium is needed for strong teeth and bones. It is an essential mineral for healthy skin and nerves. Good sources of calcium in our diets are raw nuts, sesame seeds, kelp and molasses.

   ANSWER: _____

   _____

   _____

REMEMBER Use the reading rate that meets your reading need.

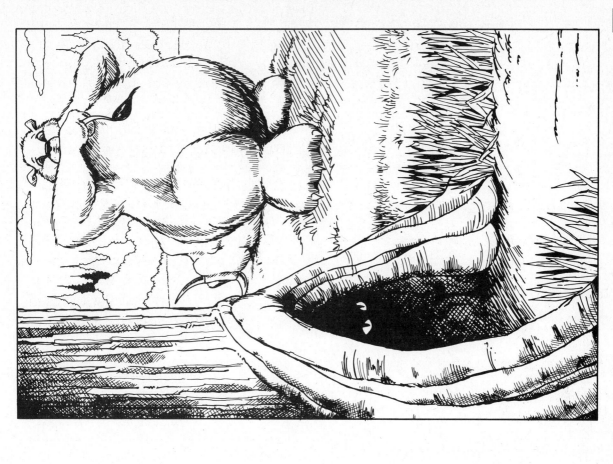

"Oh!" said Fleet-foot. This was another surprise. "What do you think he would like, Foxy?"

"Meat of some kind," she decided quickly. "He eats a huge meal, I know. I've seen that with my own eyes. You will think of something nice," she barked and scampered away.

Before long she met Bandy-legs, the Bear. He lumbered towards her and roared, "If it's not our little Foxy! Where are you off to, girl?"

"Haven't you heard, Bandy-legs? *The Lord of the Forest* has come to stay with me! His Highness is none other than Boss Cat. *The great Boss Cat!*"

"Well, I never!" gasped Bandy-legs. He was astonished. He never heard of this kind of cat. This one must be an important animal. "Would an old bear be permitted to look upon such a Highness?" he wanted to know.

"Yes, of course, you may come, but do bring a present, Bandy-legs," Foxy told him. "Boss Cat eats huge meals. Wolf has gone off to find something nice for him to eat."

"Then I'll do that, too," promised Bandy-legs, scrambling off to find a present. "I'm going to see the Highness, the Highness, the Highness," he sang to himself.

Early next morning a noise woke Boss Cat. It was a dragging, scraping sound. He was on his feet at once. Softly he crept to the opening of the den and saw a huge bear lugging a dead ox towards Foxy's place.

"Mewh!" Boss Cat said under his breath. The bear was enormous! Such strength! "Mewwh!" he mewed faintly to see behind the bear, a wolf dragging a sheep towards him.

"Well, well! Just look who is here!" bellowed the bear. He looked straight across to Foxy's den.

Boss Cat jerked his head back into the den. He was sure that the bear had seen him. This thought sent him running back to his corner, deep inside. From there, he heard only a faint rumbling of voices. How was he to know that Bandy-legs was only shouting a greeting to Fleet-foot.

"Have you come to call on His Noble Highness?" huffed Bandy-legs.

"If you mean Sir Boss Cat, then I have," said Wolf. "I have brought him a fine present. However, you were here first, Bandy-legs. You go ahead and pay your respects first. I can wait."

"No, no, not at all. *You* go first," offered Bandy-legs. "After all, you're smaller. I can wait."

"No, that won't do. You go first. *You* are bigger," argued Fleet-foot.

"I might be bigger, but you can climb trees faster than I can," mumbled Bandy-legs. He came closer to Wolf and whispered, "Don't you know that this Boss Cat is very fierce? I've heard that his claws are huge and sharp."

"I heard that too," Fleet-foot nodded unhappily.

He settled, yawned and mewed, "You may bring me my dinner."

This order flustered Foxy. She raced out of the den and did not come back until dusk. But she came back with a rabbit hanging from her jaws.

Now rabbit was Boss Cat's favorite food, next to fish. He ate with his refined cat manners and kindly left all the bones for Foxy. He never ate bones anyway.

After that he snoozed again, as a well-fed cat does. However, Foxy could not rest. She longed to spread the news about her visitor. Soon she was off, running into the forest again.

First she met Fleet-foot, the Wolf. "What's all the excitement about?" he wanted to know.

Foxy waggled from her head to her tail.

"Haven't you heard, Fleet-foot?" she gushed. "His Lordship-Highness-Catness has come to the forest. None other than Boss Cat himself is staying with me."

Fleet-foot was amazed. "Boss Cat," he murmured. He had never heard of a boss cat, but he dared not tell Foxy that. "You don't say," he blustered. "Old Boss Cat himself! I bet the king sent him and no one told *me* that he was coming." He sounded put out. "I will pay him my respects, of course," he added.

"Yes, yes, you must," nodded Foxy. "You must do so quickly. Otherwise it may be the worse for you. Boss Cat is very fierce. He has the sharpest of claws. If I were you, Fleet-foot, I would bring him a present."

He was looking about uneasily when a hare poked her head from a bush. Before she could dart back, Fleet-foot growled at her, "Come here, Squint-eye."

She came in slow hops, keeping her distance from Wolf, stood there and trembled.

"Do you know where Foxy is?" Fleet-foot asked.

The hare shook her head. How could she know where Foxy was? She certainly wasn't her friend!

Wolf ignored her shaking head. "Go and find her at once," he ordered. "Tell Foxy that Bandy-legs and Fleet-foot are at her den with gifts for His Lordship Boss."

"No, not Lordship Boss," said Bear. "Boss Cat is a Highness. The High-ness."

The next day he met a fox. She was sleek and frisky, well-fed and young. She was too young to know much about the big world outside the forest. Indeed, she was so young that she stopped short in surprise to see Boss Cat.

"Who are you?" yipped Foxy. "I've never seen an animal like you before."

Boss Cat made his back into a splendid curve. He bristled his hair until he looked twice his size and very fierce. Then he looked down his nose and said grandly, "I am the Lord of the Forest."

Foxy believed him. She bowed.

Boss Cat said, "You may call me Boss Cat."

Foxy bowed again. What could she say to this grand animal? At last she barked, "I-I didn't know that you were coming, O Great Catness. W-would you honor my humble house with your royal self?"

"Thank you, I will," said Boss Cat, hoping that he sounded proud. He certainly did, and he looked proud as well. Slowly his long neck stretched to hold his head high, and he lifted his feet high to march along with Foxy.

She pranced with excitement. Sometimes she dashed ahead, then she scampered back to walk with small dancing steps beside Boss Cat.

When they came to her den, Foxy slipped in first. She gave the place a quick dusting with her brush tail. Everything looked tidy when Boss Cat strode in to take her favorite corner for himself.

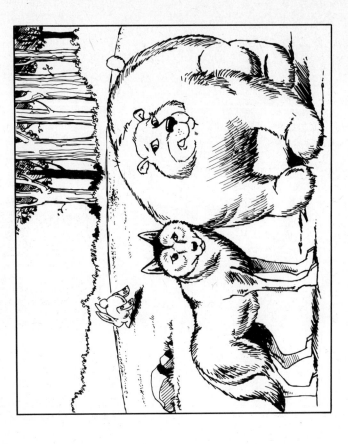

Wolf sighed and looked at Bandy-legs in a pained way. Really, that animal had muddled up his thoughts! "Well whatever he is, tell Foxy that we want to meet His Highness-Catness-Lordness-Noble Boss Cat," he said.

The little hare had gone before he was finished with his commands. As she sped away, Bandy-legs looked about with eyes that darted everywhere. He was nervous. "We really should look for a place to hide," he told Wolf from the side of this mouth. "Our Highness may come out of Foxy's den. He might think that my ox is too small for his dinner. Foxy says that His Boss Cat eats a big dinner."

By and by he saw a tumble-down hut. Most of its roof had fallen away and its walls leaned inward. The door was gone, and so were the windowpanes. Even so, Boss Cat's nose told him that it was a good place for him to stay. No person had been in this hut for a long time.

He jumped to a rafter, curled into a cat-ball for warmth, and slept very well indeed.

Although he had a new home, Boss Cat needed to hunt every day. This was not to his liking. In three days he had had little luck. It was good to have a warm sleeping place but his belly rumbled. It longed for food.

"I was Boss Cat in the town," he mewed to himself. "Maybe I can be Boss Cat in the forest."

After his struggles had started once more, a tiny rip showed in the sack. A little strip of light gleamed through it, and Boss Cat attacked the tear with new strength.

He clawed at it and it became a hole. His paw shot through the hole. Then two paws poked free. The hole was bigger. His head went through it. Now he wriggled and squirmed, shoved and twisted until his whole body slid from the sack.

Boss Cat stepped aside, then sat down in the middle of the crumpled old bag and carefully washed. He cleaned his fur of dust and oak flakes, which took a long time. After all that washing, he padded away to a path that led through the trees.

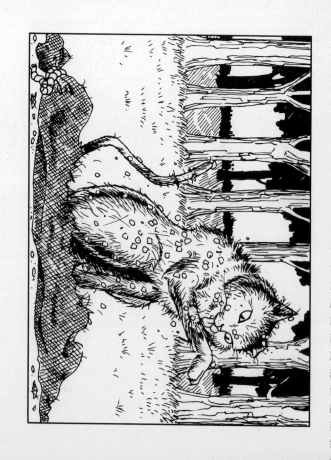

Boss Cat was too lazy and full of fish to watch for danger. He shut his eyes. He almost fell asleep.

Suddenly he was rudely shoved into something rough and bad-smelling. *Mer-yow!* He must be dreaming! His eyes opened to dusty darkness. His nose was filled with bits of fluff and stale oats. He felt hot. It was hard to breathe. He tried to struggle, but he could hardly move. He opened his claws to scratch and his legs went every which way as he was tossed over onto his back.

The best he could do was to raise a tiny, indignant yowl. Before it had ended he was swinging, bumping, and rocking about. So many bumps! Boss Cat felt sick. Sack-sick!

He was Ivan's prisoner, trapped in an old sack which Ivan had slung over his shoulder. Ivan was taking Boss Cat into the forest.

Ivan dumped the sack where the trees grew thickest.

"You stay here, Cat!" Ivan growled. "Get out if you can, but don't come back to the town."

Boss Cat kept very still, as if he were dead. He did not move until he was sure that Ivan was far away.

Now the sack bounced. It went up in the air, right off the ground. Then down! Up, down! It flopped. It rolled. Boss Cat fought the sack madly. That old bag was strong. It was harder to beat than any of the town cats.

Boss Cat's claws tore at the sack; he bit with his teeth; he wore himself out. Then he rested briefly.

"That looks like a big ox to me," decided Fleet-foot inspecting the gift.

"Perhaps it is, but Foxy did say that Boss Cat, Lord Highness eats a *lot!*" fretted Bandy-legs.

"M-maybe we'd better find a hiding place," he worried. "Let's climb this tree."

"Don't be stupid!" snapped Wolf. "You know that I can't climb a tree."

Then he began to whine. "Where can I hide, Bear? Where can I go?"

Bear shuffled his feet and scratched himself. He was thinking hard. "You could lie down there by those bushes and I'll cover you with leaves," he said slowly.

Fleet-foot flopped down at once. He looked a little happier as Bandy-legs threw leaves and twigs and sticks and bits of bark over him until he was covered. Just his nose peeked from under the pile of leaves and it could have been mistaken for a stone.

Bandy-legs was pleased with his work and he scrambled off to climb the tree. Near the top he sat in a forked branch, squirmed a little, then craned his neck to look around the forest. It wasn't long before he saw Foxy and Squint-eye trotting along the path.

Foxy marvelled at the size of the ox and the sheep but she said nothing. The cunning little thing turned on Squint-eye. "Go away now," she snapped. "The Lord of the Forest won't want you looking at him when he eats."

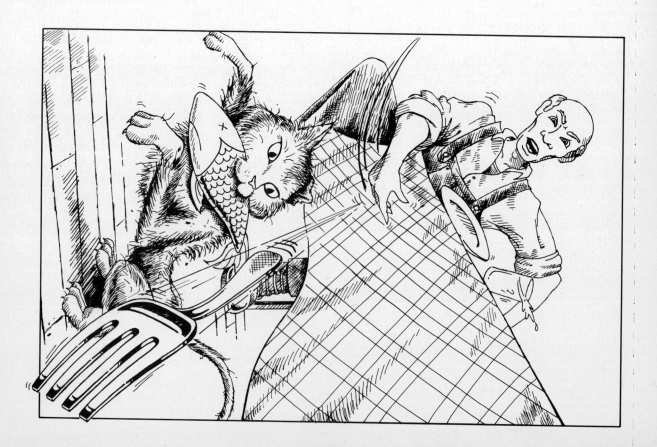

Boss Cat was quick to track the delicious smell to Ivan's kitchen. He stopped at the door with one foot raised in the air, waiting for the right moment to go in.

That moment came when Ivan's wife slid the fish from the pan to a plate. As she turned to put the plate down, Boss Cat streaked across the room to crouch under the table.

Boss Cat heard the plate arrive on the table. *Now!* One jump and he landed beside it. One snap and the fish was in his mouth. One leap and Boss Cat was out of the door again.

It all happened so fast that Ivan didn't even have time to drop his fork.

"Thief!" he shouted, as Boss Cat's long tail whipped by.

Ivan threw his fork at the flying tail. It missed, sailed through the doorway and fell into some long grass and weeds. It stayed there for weeks, so poor Ivan had lost his fork as well as his dinner.

He lost his temper next. He was furious. Fish was a rare treat for him. He was given bread and cheese instead, but he ate that every day from Monday to Sunday. Ivan was lucky if he got fish once in a whole year.

Ivan stormed. He sulked, then he brooded. He planned to catch Boss Cat. He, Ivan, would rid the town of this pest for ever.

By now Boss Cat had eaten every scrap of fish. He stretched out with the sun warming his rounded belly, and he dozed.

As the hare fled into the bushes, Foxy turned about and raced to her den. "Oh, Most Royal Boss! A great feast awaits you," she called.

"Psst! Wolf! Boss Cat Highness is coming to his dinner," hissed Bandy-legs.

"Shh! Shut-up!" warned Wolf in a low voice. "Highness will hear you."

"Aw!" grunted Bandy-legs. Now why hadn't he thought of that? He shook his head, then clutched at his branch with shock. Boss Cat had stepped from the den and Bear blinked then stared, "Aw! He's only a tiny little Highness," he muttered. "He's hardly a Highness at all!"

Boss Cat checked his surroundings and, seeing only Foxy, he stretched. He rocked on his four legs. He arched his back, straightened out and padded to the feast.

Sharp teeth and sharp claws tore at the meat. While he ate, with his delicate cat manners, he purred. Loud contented purrs.

Bandy-legs strained his ears to hear what Boss Cat was telling Foxy. The purrs sounded like horrible scoldings to him. What was Boss Cat mumbling about? Grumble-grumble-grumble! Oh, glory! Boss Cat must be saying. "Smmmmmallll, *smmmmmallll, smalllllll!*"

Bear was so alarmed that he forgot to stay silent. "Wolf! His Royalness is *not* pleased!" he called. "He says my ox is too small, but he's not much bigger than Squint-eye himself! Wolf, what will he say about your sheep?"

Boss Cat lifted his head. Bear's rumbling voice sounded like far away thunder, but since he knew nothing of bears, he went on eating.

But Fleet-foot bristled. His sheep too small! Ridiculous! It would take a wolf two days to eat it. That Boss Cat must be some kind of monster. A greedy-guts! A glutton! He lifted his head to glare at the feasting gobble-jaws.

Leaves rustled.

Boss Cat stopped eating to listen. He thought, "Ah, a town mouse. I haven't chased one for ages."

There were more rustlings over there in those leaves. Boss Cat's ears pricked to points and even his crumpled ear straightened. His green eyes narrowed to glinting slits until he couldn't resist the mouse sounds any longer. Boss Cat sprang with opened claws. Down! He dropped on Fleet-foot's soft nose.

Fleet-foot yelped and leapt from his leafy cover. His howls were awful to hear as he bounded away to the thickest part of the forest.

Boss Cat yowled with fright and sprinted to Bear's tree. He clawed up the trunk, jumping from branch to branch. In no time he was just under the place where Bear's fat bottom draped over his branch like a huge bees' nest.

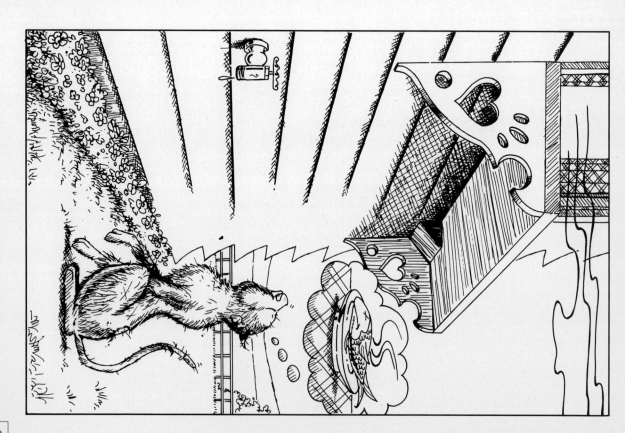

Outside in the barns, the mice romped and dined from the grain bags in broad daylight. The youngest ones swung on the cows' tails. And all the mice grew very, very fat.

Even Boss Cat hardly ever bothered to chase them. He could find a better dinner, without the trouble of catching it, by raiding the nearest kitchen.

No one loved Boss Cat, and Boss Cat didn't think much of anyone. Indeed, he didn't seem to like people at all. If a person tried to touch him, Boss Cat hissed and spat. He could kick and scratch, too.

To show that he didn't care two whiskers for people, Boss Cat marched by them with his tail in the air.

Boss Cat's life might have gone on in this lonely way, except that one day, he wanted Ivan's dinner. It happened to be fresh fish.

Ivan's wife had cooked the fish in butter until it sizzled golden and crisp. The fine fishy smell drifted from the stove and out of the kitchen window to Boss Cat. He sniffed it with delight—it was a long time since he had eaten fish.

A moment later, frantic claws pricked through bear's fur to bare skin.

Ooowah! Ourrh! Bandy-legs crashed out of the tree! Down he went and branches, twigs and leaves hit the ground with him. He lay as flat as a bearskin rug. His tongue hung out. His eyes bulged. He thought he was dead. Then he felt that every one of his bones was broken. Really, he was too fat for that to have happened, but he moaned and groaned.

Once, there was a thin, black cat and no one loved him. His green eyes were like slits in his sharply pointed face. This cat had only one ear. The other hung from the side of his head like a crumpled rag. It was a sign that he had been in too many cat fights.

He had other scars of battle, too. His dull fur looked as if it had been chewed by moths. Poor cat! He looked as if he had been beaten many times, but don't you believe it!

He was a wild cat, a wicked old tom, a fast-moving bundle of spitting fur. That's what the people in the town said. He was the boss cat for miles around.

Every other cat feared or hated Boss Cat.

So did the people who owned those fat house cats and skinny farm cats, because at some time Boss Cat had fought each one. So now the town cats were frightened to leave their sleeping places on the stoves. They stayed home night and day, and Boss Cat had them so scared that they even gave up chasing mice.

The little squeakers and nibblers had grown as bold as lions. They ran about the houses as they pleased; they nested in boxes, drawers and cupboards; and they held crumb parties beside the stoves, right under the cats' noses.

Looking up, he saw Boss Cat swaying on a branch. He looked like an angry ball of black fur. Green eyes glared down at him, lips curled into a fierce snarl.

Then, worst of all, Boss Cat spat and hissed.

It was too much for Bandy-legs. He heaved himself to his feet and stumbled away. Bandy-legs was a fear-filled, trembling bag of shabby fur.

Foxy was circling the tree trying to see Boss Cat.

"Are you safe and sound?" she yipped.

"Of coursssse!" he told her with the tiny trill of a purr.

"I thought you were hurt, little friend," Foxy said then.

Friend! She had called him *friend!* Foxy liked him enough to care about him! Boss Cat slithered down the tree.

Soon they shared a peaceful dinner. It was the first of many which they would eat together.

Before long, Boss Cat looked sleek and handsome. At last he had a friend. She didn't mind his looks or habits and she *wanted* to be his friend. In her cunning foxy way, she loved him.

Boss Cat had landed on his feet. He was a lucky black cat. Very lucky!

As for the other two, Bandy-legs and Fleet-foot, they stayed far away from the part of the forest where the little Highness-Catness-Royalest-Noble Boss lived for ever more.

Boss Cat

Jean Chapman